双双中文教材(19)
Chinese Language and Culture Course

中国历史(上) History of China (I)

王双双 编著

北京大学出版社
PEKING UNIVERSITY PRESS

图书在版编目（CIP）数据

中国历史.上/王双双 编著.—北京：北京大学出版社，2007.9
（双双中文教材19）
ISBN 978-7-301-08704-6

Ⅰ.中… Ⅱ.王… Ⅲ.汉语-对外汉语教学-教材 Ⅳ.H195.4

中国版本图书馆CIP数据核字（2005）第075457号

书　　名：	中国历史（上）
著作责任者：	王双双　编著
英 文 翻 译：	王亦兵
责 任 编 辑：	邓晓霞　孙　娴
标 准 书 号：	ISBN 978-7-301-08704-6/ H·1440
出 版 发 行：	北京大学出版社
地　　　址：	北京市海淀区成府路205号 100871
网　　　址：	http://www.pup.cn
电　　　话：	邮购部 62752015　发行部62750672　编辑部62752028　出版部62754962
电 子 信 箱：	zpup@pup.pku.edu.cn
印 　刷 　者：	北京宏伟双华印刷有限公司
经 　销 　者：	新华书店
	889毫米×1194毫米　16开本　10.5印张　119千字
	2007年9月第1版　2022年3月第6次印刷
定　　　价：	85.00元（含课本、练习册和CD-ROM盘一张）

未经许可，不得以任何方式复制或抄袭本书之部分或全部内容。
版权所有，侵权必究
举报电话：（010）62752024
电子信箱：fd@pup.pku.edu.cn

前言

《双双中文教材》是一套专门为海外青少年编写的中文课本，是我在美国八年的中文教学实践基础上编写成的。在介绍这套教材之前，请读一首小诗：

> 一双神奇的手，
> 推开一扇窗。
> 一条神奇的路，
> 通向灿烂的中华文化。
>
> 鲍凯文 鲍维江
> 1998年

鲍维江和鲍凯文姐弟俩是美国生美国长的孩子，也是我的学生。1998年冬，他们送给我的新年贺卡上的小诗，深深地打动了我的心。我把这首诗看成我文化教学的"回声"。我要传达给海外每位中文老师：我教给他们（学生）中国文化，他们思考了、接受了、回应了。这条路走通了！

语言是交际的工具，更是一种文化和一种生活方式，所以学习中文也就离不开中华文化的学习。汉字是一种古老的象形文字，她从远古走来，带有大量的文化信息，但学起来并不容易。使学生增强兴趣、减小难度，走出苦学汉字的怪圈，走进领悟中华文化的花园，是我编写这套教材的初衷。

学生不论大小，天生都有求知的欲望，都有欣赏文化美的追求。中华文化本身是魅力十足的。把这宏大而玄妙的文化，深入浅出地，有声有色地介绍出来，让这迷人的文化如涓涓细流，一点一滴地渗入学生们的心田，使学生们逐步体味中国文化，是我编写这套教材的目的。

为此我将汉字的学习放入文化介绍的流程之中同步进行，让同学们在学中国地理的同时，学习汉字；在学中国历史的同时，学习汉字；在学中国哲学的同时，学习汉字；在学中国科普文选的同时，学习汉字……

这样的一种中文学习，知识性强，趣味性强；老师易教，学生易学。当学生们合上书本时，他们的眼前是中国的大好河山，是中国五千年的历史和妙不可言的哲学思维，是奔腾的现代中国……

总之，他们了解了中华文化，就会探索这片土地，热爱这片土地，就会与中国结下情缘。

最后我要衷心地感谢所有热情支持和帮助我编写教材的老师、家长、学生、朋友和家人，特别是老同学唐玲教授、何茜老师、我姐姐王欣欣编审和她的儿子杨眉及我女儿Uta Guo年复一年的鼎力相助。可以说这套教材是大家努力的结果。

王双双
2005年5月8日

说 明

《双双中文教材》是一套专门为海外学生编写的中文教材。它是由美国加州王双双老师和中国专家学者共同努力，在海外多年的实践中编写出来的。全书共20册，识字量2500个，包括了从识字、拼音、句型、短文的学习，到初步的较系统的中国文化的学习。教材大体介绍了中国地理、历史、哲学等方面的丰富内容，突出了中国文化的魅力。课本知识面广，趣味性强，深入浅出，易教易学。

这套教材体系完整、构架灵活、使用面广。学生可以从零起点开始，一直学完全部课程20册；也可以将后11册（10～20册）的九个文化专题和第五册（汉语拼音）单独使用，这样便于高中和大学开设中国哲学、地理、历史等专门课程以及假期班、短期中国文化班、拼音速成班使用，符合美国AP中文课程的目标和基本要求。

本书是《双双中文教材》的第十九册，由王双双在杨东梁先生（中国人民大学图书馆馆长、清史研究所所长）的指导和帮助之下，在海外中文教学实践的基础上编写而成。全书语言简单，概要地介绍了中国从远古时期到唐代上半叶的历史知识。学生们通过学习，不仅能较系统地了解中国历史，中文的识字数量和语汇水平也将得到明显的提高。

考虑到海外汉语历史教学的特殊性，为了便利教学，本书的编写采取了化繁为简的原则，历史年代表中没有以王朝兴起的年代为它的起始年代，而是以它正式替代前朝的时间为准，如：秦、清等朝；或者以正式设立本国号的年代为准，如：辽、元等朝。特此说明。

编者

课程设置

一年级	中文课本(第一册)	中文课本(第二册)	中文课本(第三册)
二年级	中文课本(第四册)	中文课本(第五册)	中文课本(第六册)
三年级	中文课本(第七册)	中文课本(第八册)	中文课本(第九册)
四年级	中国成语故事	中国地理常识	
五年级	中国古代故事	中国神话传说	
六年级	中国古代科学技术	中国文学欣赏	
七年级	中国诗歌欣赏	中文科普阅读	
八年级	中国古代哲学	中国历史(上)	
九年级	中国历史(下)	小说阅读, 中文SAT II	
十年级	中文SAT II (强化班)	小说阅读,中文SAT II考试	

目录

第一课	中国最早的人类	1
第二课	夏、商、西周	10
第三课	春秋与战国	20
第四课	秦	31
第五课	西汉	41
第六课	东汉	51
第七课	三国鼎立	60
第八课	两晋、南北朝	70
第九课	隋	80
第十课	唐（上）	88
生字表		99
生词表		101
中国历史朝代年表		105

第一课

中国最早的人类

中国位于欧亚大陆的东方,地势西高东低,北、西、西南三面被高原、山脉环绕,东面是海洋,形成一个相对独立的环境。

考古证明,早在170万年以前,中国大地上已有了原始人类。1965年,科学家在云南省元谋县发现了两颗170万年前的人牙化石和这些人制造、使用的石器,还有烧过的木炭屑和兽骨等,因此,这些原始人被称为"元谋人"。

1963年,科学家在陕西省蓝田县发现了80万年前的猿人头骨化石,这些原始人类被称为"蓝田人"。

从1927年起,考古学家在北京市周口店地区陆续发现了六个50万年前的古人类头骨化石、很多人牙和猿人骨骼(gé)。这些原始人类被称为"北京人"。他们生活的山洞里有很厚的堆积物,其中有"北京人"用火的灰烬以及大量的石器和骨角器。

山顶洞人头骨化石
(1933年北京周口店出土)

1933年,科学家们又在北京周口店龙骨山顶的山洞里,发现

山顶洞人复原胸像

了18,000年前的三个完整的人类头骨化石，科学家称他们为"山顶洞人"。"山顶洞人"不但制造石器、骨器，而且制造骨制的装饰品，这说明"山顶洞人"已经有了爱美的观念。"山顶洞人"不但会用火，还会人工取火，会用兽皮做衣服。"山顶洞人"后期是这样生活的：一个家族的几十个人一起居住，一起劳动，一起吃饭。这种生活集体叫做氏族公社。

大约6,000多年前，在黄河中下游地区，氏族公社繁荣起来。他们的活动以农业为主，种田、饲养家畜、盖房、烧制陶器和纺织。这个时期是母系氏族社会，有同一个始祖母，如半坡氏族（在今陕西省）。

大约5,000多年前，黄河流域形成了父系氏族，人们开始过着有夫妻的家庭生活。之后几个氏族组成一个部落，几个部落组成部落联盟。相传4,600年前，黄河边上强大的黄帝部落和炎帝部落联合起来打败了蚩（chī）尤部

半坡氏族单鱼纹盆

半坡遗址

落之后，炎、黄两大部落合并在一起，形成了华夏族。这就是为什么说中华民族是"炎黄子孙"的原因。

但是，中国古代的文明不仅仅发源于黄河流域，在长江流域、华南和西南地区、北方草原地区，都发现了氏族社会人类居住的遗址。各地的氏族部落逐渐发展，建立联系，共同创造了中华民族远古的文化。

山顶洞人的骨针
（1933年北京周口店出土）

生词

dú lì 独立	independent		guān niàn 观念	sense
kǎo gǔ 考古	archeology		shì zú 氏族	gentile
yuán móu 元谋	Yuanmou (a county in Yunnan Province)		fán róng 繁荣	prosperous; flourish
yuán rén 猿人	ape man		bù luò 部落	tribe
lù xù 陆续	in succession		lián méng 联盟	alliance
huī jìn 灰烬	ash		lián hé 联合	unite
wán zhěng 完整	complete		yí zhǐ 遗址	site; ruins; relics
zhuāng shì 装饰	decorate			

听写

装饰　考古　联合　独立　观念　陆续　氏族　遗址

完整　元谋　*猿人

注：*号以后的字词为选做题，后同。

比一比

装 { 装饰品　服装　假装 }

联 { 联合　联盟　联系 }

合 { 合并　合作　合适 }

续 { 陆续　继续　连续 }

独 { 独立　单独　孤独 }

氏 { 氏族　姓氏 }

遗 { 遗址　遗迹 }

址 { 住址　地址 }

字词运用

完整

请把这个故事完整地复述一遍。

陆续
同学们陆续走进了教室。

观念
中国有些地方还存在着重男轻女的旧观念。

观点
对于同一个电影,我和妈妈的观点就不一样。

观看
我在北京观看了大卫的魔术表演。

回答问题

1. 中国最早的原始人类出现在多少万年以前?
2. 为什么说中华民族是"炎黄子孙"?

词语解释

母系氏族社会——氏族社会早期，由于以农业、饲养家畜和管理家务为主，又由于群婚，子女只能确认生母，于是女子在经济上和社会上的地位高，能做主。

阅读

黄帝的故事

相传，黄帝姓姬（另一说姓公孙），名轩辕，生活在大约4,600年前。那时候黄河边住着许多部落，其中住在黄土高原上的黄帝和炎帝部落比较先进、强大；而居住在山东的九黎部落虽然强大，但落后得多，他们的首领叫蚩尤。

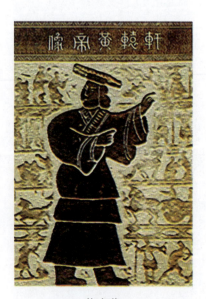

黄帝像

后来炎、黄、蚩尤三大部落发生了战争。先是炎帝与蚩尤为了争夺黄河下游平原地区，发生了战争。这里人口众多，土地肥沃。结果蚩尤胜了。于是炎帝向黄帝求救。黄帝和炎帝带领族人磨制石刀、石斧，组成了一支用虎、豹、熊等猛兽做名字的部队；他们让虎队的首

领身披虎皮，豹队的首领身披豹皮。而蚩尤呢，他有81个兄弟，个个都十分勇猛。

炎黄部落和九黎部落的大战终于爆发了。一边是由蚩尤和他的81个兄弟在前面，一边是黄帝和炎帝的虎、豹、熊队做先锋。这一仗打得十分激烈，最后蚩尤战败被杀，九黎部落并入了炎黄部落。

打败蚩尤后，炎帝和黄帝为争当部落联盟的首领，又打了一仗，炎帝失败。于是两部落合并，其他的部落也纷纷加入。

传说黄帝还是一个发明家。他教人们盖房子、养家畜、种五谷。此外，他还发明了车和船等交通工具。据说是黄帝的妻子嫘祖发明了养蚕，教人们把丝织成绸子做衣服。黄帝的史官仓颉创造了文字，而他的乐师制定了音律。总之，黄帝、炎帝两个部落合并后，在黄河流域长期生活下来，成为华夏族的主干，中华民族以黄帝为祖先，中国人也自称"炎黄子孙"。

生词

jī 姬	Ji (surname)	chī yóu 蚩尤	Chiyou (name)
xuān yuán 轩辕	Xuanyuan (name)	pī 披	wear
jiǔ lí 九黎	Jiuli (tribe)	léi zǔ 嫘祖	Leizu (name)

Lesson One

The Earliest Human Beings in China

China is located in the east of the Eurasia and the general topography is high in the west and low in the east. The country is surrounded by either plateaus or mountain ranges in three sides of the north, the west and the southwest, and is bordered by the sea in its east. Therefore, it is a relatively independent land.

According to archeological research, more than 1.7 million years ago, there were hominid species living in China. In 1965, scientists found two pieces of human teeth fossil that can be dated back to 1.7 million years ago in Yuanmo county of Yunnan Province, together with flintware they made and used as well as burned charcoal ashes and animal bones. The hominid was then named Yuanmo Man.

In 1963, scientists discovered in Lantian County of Shaanxi Province the fossils of hominid skull that can be dated back to 800,000 years ago and named them Lantian Man.

Since 1927, archeologists have found in Zhoukoudian of Beijing a total of six skull fossils of ape man that can be dated back to a half million years ago, numerous teeth and bone fossils. This species was named Peking Man. A large pile of deposit has been found in the cave they used to live, among which ashes and a large amount of flintware as well as bone and horn wares were discovered.

In 1933, three complete fossils skulls were found in a cave on top of the Longgu Mountain in Beijing Zhoukoudian. The skulls can be dated back to 18,000 years ago and the scientists named these people Upper Cave Man (Shandingdong Man). They not only made flintware, bone wares but also decorative bone articles, showing that the Upper Cave Man had the sense of beauty. They used fire and could make fire themselves. They also made themselves clothes from animal skin. During the late stage, dozens of family members lived together, labored together and dined together. This family-based group is later known as gentile community.

About 6,000 BC, gentile communities became universal in the middle and downstream area along the Yellow River. The leading activity was agriculture; they farmed land, raised livestock, built houses, made pottery, and weaved. It was the matriarchal society at that time and people were descendents of the same original grandmother, Banpo Clan (located in today's Shaanxi Province) is one of them.

About 5,000 years ago, patriarchal society firstly appeared in the area along the Yellow River and people began to settle down for monogamous family life. Later on, several clans formed one tribe and several tribes created a tribe alliance. It is said that about 4,600 years ago, two tribes led by Emperor Huang and Emperor Yan respectively united and defeated the Chiyou Tribe. The two tribes united and created the national of Huaxia, which is the reason why Chinese call themselves the descendents of Yan and Huang.

But the Yellow River Area is not the only origin for ancient Chinese civilization, people found in the Yangtze River Area, South China, Southwest Area, and the grassland in the north the sites proving ancient people used to live in these places. The tribes located in different areas expanded gradually their influence and joined hands in creating ancient Chinese civilization.

Legends about Emperor Huang

According to the legends, the surname of Emperor Huang was Ji (some believe that his family name was Gongsun) and his first name was Xuanyuan. He lived about 4,600 years ago when there were many tribes along the Yellow River, among which two tribes led by Emperor Huang and Emperor Yan were the most powerful. The Jiuli Tribe residing in Shandong Province was also strong; but it was no match for the tribes led by Yan and Huang. The chieftain of the Jiuli Tribe was Chiyou.

Later on, a war broke out among these three tribes. Firstly, Emperor Yan fought with Chiyou for the plain in the downstream area along the Yellow River. The area was dense populated and the land was extremely fertile there. Chiyou won the war and Emperor Yan turned to Emperor Huang for help. Emperors Huang and Yan organized armies named after tiger, leopard and bear and their soldiers were armed with stone knives and stone axes. The leader of the tiger army wore tiger skin and the leader of the leopard army wore leopard skin. Chiyou had 81 brothers and all of them were brave fighters.

A great war finally broke out between the tribes led by Emperors Yan and Huang and the Jiuli Tribe. Chiyou and his 81 brothers led the army to fight with the tiger, leopard and bear armies of Emperors Huang and Yan. The fighting was fierce; finally Chiyou was defeated and killed, his Jiuli Tribe was merged by the Yan and Huan.

After defeating Chiyou, Emperor Yan and Emperor Huang fought for the chieftain of the tribe union and Emperor Yan was defeated. Two tribes merged and joined by other small tribes.

According to the legends, Emperor Huang was an inventor and he taught people build houses, raise livestock, plant five kinds of cereals, cook with fire, and change the original nomadic and hunting life. In addition, he invented several means of transportation including carriage and boat. It is said that his wife Luozu was the first to rear silkworms and taught people to weave silk and to make silk clothing. Cangjie was the historiographer of Emperor Huang and he created Chinese characters. The musician of Emperor Huang created musical scale. After two tribes led by Emperor Huang and Emperor Yan unified, people began to settle down in the Yellow River Area and they were the core of the entire Huaxia Nation. Chinese honor Emperor Huang as their ancestor and call themselves the descendents of Yan and Huang.

第二课

夏、商、西周

黄帝之后,黄河常有水灾。尧、舜、禹三个首领先后带领大家治理洪水。经过多年的努力,禹带领人们终于治服了洪水。那时部落首领老了之后,由大家推举有才能的人当新首领。这种制度叫"禅(shàn)让"。尧、舜、禹都是通过禅让当上首领的。

大禹像

禹因治水有功,当了部落联盟的首领,建立了夏朝(约公元前21世纪—约前17世纪)。在他的领导下,人们的生活和平、安定。禹晚年的时候推举伯益为继承人,但禹死后,他的儿子启打破了禅让制,开始了中国历史上子承父位的世袭王朝。启统治的夏是一个奴隶制国家,中国从原始社会进入了奴隶社会。

夏的疆土主要在黄

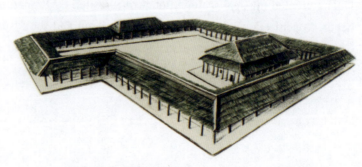

二里头夏代建筑复原图

河两岸，现在的河南、山西一带。国王称"天子"。夏朝建立了军队，制定了法律，并且还设立了监狱。

夏的土地属于国有，奴隶种的是公田。人们能够制造青铜器，造酒，生产美丽的玉器。夏朝开始制定历法，定一年为十二个月。直到现在，中国人还在使用夏历。夏历也叫"农历"或"阴历"。这些都说明中国历史已经进入了文明时期。

夏朝统治了471年，最后一个国王桀(jié)是个暴君，他只知道吃喝玩乐，欺压百姓，引起人们的不满，最后被商灭亡。

商住在黄河下游，他们的祖先因和禹一起治水而得到商地。商渐渐强大起来，后来发兵消灭了夏，建立了商朝。

商朝（约前17世纪—约前11世纪）的势力范围比夏大，人口有几百万。商朝国力强大，制定了成文的法律并拥有几万人的庞大军队。

商朝的土地为国有，大批奴隶在农田集体工作。当时的青铜铸造业已十分发达。出土的商代青铜器司母戊(wù)鼎重875公斤，制作水平相当高。商代出现了刻在龟甲、兽骨上的文字，后人称它为"甲骨文"。商朝的人还积累了不少早期天文学的知识。

司母戊鼎（商）

商朝最后的国王纣十分残暴，人们都痛恨他。商有个属国叫周，首领周武王率领他的军队攻打商纣王，在牧野打败了商军，建立周朝。商王朝灭亡。

西周（约前11世纪—约前771年）的势力范围东到海滨，西到现在的甘肃东部，南到长江以南，北到现今的河北等地。西周时，周天子把土地分给王公贵族，建立了许多诸侯国。当时的手工业主要是青铜铸造，青铜器上常常铸刻着文字，这些文字被后人称作金文，有些金文记录了西周历史上的重大事件。

西周末年，王室内部互相争斗，周幽王被杀。太子宜臼继承王位，就是周平王。他将都城向东迁移到今天的洛阳，建立了东周。

生词

尧 yáo	Yao (name)	残暴 cán bào	cruel
启 qǐ	Qi (name)	率领 shuài lǐng	lead
奴隶 nú lì	slave	海滨 hǎi bīn	seaside
监狱 jiān yù	prison	诸侯 zhū hóu	vassal
铸造 zhù zào	cast	周幽王 zhōu yōu wáng	Emperor Youwang of Zhou
水平 shuǐ píng	technique; level		Dynasty

听写

奴隶　海滨　率领　尧　积累　属于　首领　辽宁

监狱　水平　*残暴

比一比

治 { 治服 / 治理 / 治病 　　首 { 首领 / 首都 　　朝 { 王朝 / 朝鲜 　　蓝（蓝天）/ 监（监狱）

属 { 属于 / 金属 　　疆 { 疆土 / 新疆 　　袭 { 世袭 / 袭击 　　铸（铸造）/ 寿（寿命）

字词运用

积累

知识是年年月月坚持学习，积累而成的。

劳累

过分劳累会损害身体健康。

属于

这支表演队不属于我们学校,属于一个俱乐部(jù)。

回答问题

1. 请说出夏、商、周三个朝代的年代。

2. 夏、商、周时期最主要的手工业是什么?

3. 请解释"禅让"一词。

词语解释

世袭——指帝位、爵(jué)位等世代相传。

历法——用年、月、日计算时间的方法。

欺压——欺负、压迫。

庞大——很大。

积累——逐渐汇集,积少成多。

首领——指某些集团的领导人。

阅读

甲骨文

甲骨文是古代刻在龟甲或兽骨上的文字，也是3,000多年前中国商代使用的文字。商朝灭亡后，祖庙和档案馆都倒塌了。经过漫长的岁月，废墟又被覆盖上厚厚的黄土，所有的东西都被埋没了。以后几乎没人再知道那时的文字了。

直到1899年，著名学者王懿荣买到一些被当作中药的"龙骨"，发现上面刻的纹理很像汉字。经过研究，他发现这些"龙骨"上的文字是商代占卜的卜辞。后来这些骨片到了他的好朋友刘鹗手中。1903年刘鹗出版了第一本介绍甲骨文的书，名为《铁云藏龟》，书中收集了1,058片甲骨，在当时引起很大的轰动。

甲骨文（河南安阳出土）

一些文字学家和文物商人了解到这些"龙骨"的价值，马上赶往河南省安阳市郊外的小屯。3,000多年前，那里曾经是商朝的国都。小屯附近有个大土堆，当地的农民在那里挖"龙骨"，拿到药店里去卖。从古代开始，他们一直这样做，但是没有人注意到上面的文字。有人甚至磨掉上面的字使"龙骨"光滑，更容易卖。

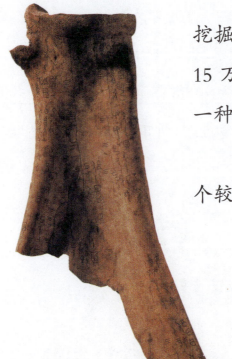

甲骨文

1928年，科学家对小屯进行了科学性的挖掘，发现了大量甲骨。至今，已出土甲骨15万片。古文字学家认识到甲骨上面的字是一种比西周金文还要早的文字。

甲骨文共有约4,500多单字，已经形成一个较完整的文字体系，而且有了"主语-谓语-宾语"的次序。甲骨文已有了从一到十和百千万等13个记数单字，使用十进制记数，出现过四位数，较大的数是30,000；已有奇数、偶数、倍数的概念。从甲骨文上可以知道，当时已经有了完整的六十甲子①和历法。甲骨文的发现，使人们更真实地了解了3,000多年前商朝人的社会生活情况。但是时至今日，还有2/3的甲骨文文字，人们无法确切知道它们的含义。

---

① 甲子——古代用干支来表示年、月、日的次序，周而复始，循(xún)环使用。60年为一甲子。

生词

dàng àn 档案	archives	bǔ cí 卜辞	oracle inscription shown on tortoiseshells
fèi xū 废墟	ruin		or animal bones of Shang Dynasty
liú è 刘鹗	Liu E (*name*)	xiǎo tún 小屯	Xiaotun (*village*)
wáng yì róng 王懿荣	Wang Yirong (*name*)	jī shù 奇数	odd number
zhān bǔ 占卜	divination	ǒu shù 偶数	even number
		gài niàn 概念	concept

 English Translation

Lesson Two

Three Dynasties of Xia, Shang, and Western Zhou

After the reign of Emperor Huang, people suffered frequently from the flood caused by the Yellow River. Accordingly, three emperors of Yao, Shun, and Yu led people to fight against the flood. After years of efforts, Yu led people and conquer the flood. At that time, when a chieftain became old, a most talented man would be recommended and this system was known as Shan-rang. Yao, Shun and Yu all benefited from the system.

Yu was chosen to be the chieftain for his achievements in fighting against the flood and founded the Xia Dynasty (about 21st Century BC-17th Century BC). Under his reign, people enjoyed a peaceful and stable life. When Yu was getting old, he recommended Boyi as his successor. But after Yu died, his son Qi succeeded the throne and founded the first slave state in China. China moves from primitive society to slave society.

The territory of the Xia Dynasty included mainly today's Henan and Shanxi Province along both banks of the Yellow River. The emperor was known as the son of God (*tianzi*) and the state organized army, made a legal system and built prisons.

During the Xia Dynasty, all the land belonged to the state and the slaves planted on allocated public farming land. People were capable of making bronze ware, brewing wine, producing beautiful jade ware. During the Xia Dynasty, people started to create calendar and divided one year into twelve months. Till now, Chinese still use Xia calendar, which is also known as Chinese traditional calendar or lunar calendar. China has entered civilization period.

Xia Dynasty lasts 471 years and the last emperor Jie was a tyrant. Jie was an expert of noting except for dining, drinking, having fun and bullying people. He was so resented by people and was finally overcome by Shang.

Shang people lived in the downstream area along the Yellow River and their ancestors got the area for helping Emperor Yu in his water control project. Shang gradually developed and then sent army to defeat the official army of Xia Dynasty and founded Shang Dynasty.

The territory of Shang (about 17th Century BC-about 11th Century BC) was much larger than that of Xia; its population reached several million and the state was powerful in strength, had written law and an army with dozens of thousands of soldiers.

During the Shang Dynasty, all the land belonged to the state and was planted by slaves collectively. The bronze casting industry was developed at the time and the excavated bronze Simuwu cauldron weighs 875kg, which indicates that the bronze manufacturing technique at that time was very high. The language used by people during the Shang Dynasty is known as "Jiaguwen", for they were inscribed on tortoise shells or animal bones; Shang people also accumulated early astronomical knowledger.

Zhou was the last emperor of the Shang Dynasty and he was extremely cruel to slaves; people hated him very much. Then the chieftain King Wu of the Kingdom of Zhou subordinated to Shang sent army to fight with and defeat the army of the Emperor Zhou of Shang Dynasty at Muye. The Western Zhou was founded and the Shang Dynasty finally collapsed.

The territory of the Western Zhou (about 11th Century BC-about 771BC) extended to the sea in the east, to the eastern Gansu Province in the west, to the southern part of the Yangtze River in the south and to today's Hebei Province in the north. During the Western Zhou, the emperor distributed the land to royal and noble family members and they founded many vassal states. The dominating handicraft industry at that time was the casting of bronze utensils, which were generally cast or inscribed with characters, known as Jinwen today, recording the important events during the reign of the Western Zhou.

At the end of the Western Zhou, there was internal fighting within the royal family and Emperor Youwang was killed. The crown prince Yijiu took the throne, known as Emperor Pingwang. He moved the capital eastward to today's Luoyang and founded the Eastern Zhou.

Jiaguwen

Jiaguwen is an ancient language inscribed on tortoise shells or animal bones and the common language during the Shang Dynasty about 3,000 years ago. After the collapse of the Shang Dynasty, the ancestral temple and the archive were both collapsed. Long time passed, the ruins were covered by a thick layer of loess brought by flood. All were buried and nobody knew anything about Jiaguwen.

Until 1899 when a famous scholar Wang Yirong bought some "dragon bones" as traditional Chinese medicine, he discovered that the inscriptions on them looked like Chinese character. After research, he believed that these inscriptions on "dragon bones" were oracle inscription during Shang Dynasty. Later on, these bones were in possession of Liu E, one of his best friends. In 1903, Liu E published his *Tieyun Canggui*, the first book introducing Jiaguwen. The book collected 1,058 shells and bones, causing a big stir at the time.

Hearing about the value of these "dragon bones", the perceptive linguistics and smart businessmen dealing with cultural relics rushed to a small village located in suburban area of Anyang, Henan Province, for this used to be the capital city of the Shang Dynasty more than 3,000 years ago. There was a large pile of earth deposit near the village and the poverty-stricken farmers would go there digging for "dragon bones" and sell them to medical stores. They had been doing this since ancient times but none of them ever noticed the inscriptions on the bones. Someone even rubbed away the inscriptions on the bones to make them smoother for a good price.

In 1928, a scientific excavation was carried out in the village and a large amount of bones and shells were discovered. Up to now, more than 150,000 pieces of shells and bones have been excavated and then scholars studying ancient languages realized that the characters inscribed on these shells and bones were even earlier than the inscriptions on bronze objects used during the Western Zhou.

There are about 4,500 single characters found in the ancient inscriptions on animal bones or tortoise shells, which have already formed a relatively complete language system. These characters are arranged in the order of the subject, the predicate, and the object. We can also find 13 single numerical characters standing for one to ten as well as one hundred, one thousand, and ten thousand. We also know that people living in the Shang Dynasty adopted decimal system and knew the concepts of odd number, even number and multiple. There had been four digits numbers and one of the largest number is thirty thousand. People studying these ancient inscriptions on animal bones or tortoise shells also know that there was complete cycle of sixty years and calendar at that time. The discovery of Jiaguwen enables people to understand more about the social lives of people during the Shang Dynasty more than 3,000 years ago. But until today, we cannot understand the meaning of two thirds of these characters.

第三课

春秋与战国

东周(前770—前256年)，前后500多年。一般把这段历史分为两个时期：春秋时期（前770—前476年）和战国时期（前475—前221年）。

春秋时期的特点是诸侯争霸。春秋初年，有100多个诸侯国，为了争夺土地和人口，诸侯国之间常常发生混战。周天子的势力已经很弱，经济上、政治上都要依靠强大诸侯的支持。最开始称霸的是齐国的国君齐桓(huán)公。齐是东方大国，齐桓公任用管仲(zhòng)为相，改革内政，国家强大起来。公元前651年，齐桓公邀请各个诸侯举行盛大的盟会，成为盟主。后来晋国在晋文公时期强大起来，

成为中原霸主。楚国国君楚庄王和秦国的秦穆(mù)公，也都是争霸者。争霸的还有中原的宋国和长江下游的吴、越两国。

公元前475年，开始了战国时期。经过360多年的战争，到战国时期只剩了20多个诸侯国，其中以齐、楚、燕、韩、赵、魏、秦七国最强，称为"战国七雄"。这七个国家所以强大，是因为它们都进行了不同程度的改革，特别是秦国。秦孝公任用商鞅(yāng)实行变法：废除官爵世袭制度，奖励作战有功的人；废除分封制①，设立41个县，委派官员管理；废除"井田"②，实行土地私有，奖励耕织；统一度量衡等等。后来，商鞅虽然被贵族杀害，新法却得到推行，为秦统一中国打下了基础。

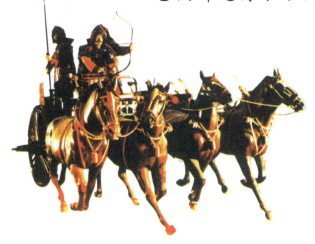

战国战车（复原模型）

战国时期，通过变法，土地可以自由买卖，农民生产热情提

---

① 分封制——一种政治制度。君主把土地分给宗亲和功臣，让他们统治自己的领地。

② 井田制——商、周实行的一种奴隶主的土地国有制，这个制度强迫奴隶在公田上无偿(cháng)劳动。

高；又普遍使用了铁制农具，新修建了许多水利工程，如：魏国引漳(zhāng)河水灌溉田地；秦国修建了都江堰和郑国渠，使农业生产发展很快。手工业方面，冶铁、漆器、造船等都具有相当的规模，工艺水平较高。同时，城市人口增加，货币大量流通，商人成为一支重要的社会力量。这时候，中国进入了封建社会。

春秋时期铜剑
（1965年湖北出土）

春秋战国时期是一个战争不断，社会大动荡、大变化的时期，也是一个思想文化大发展的时期。诸子百家纷纷提出自己的学说和主张。其中孔子、孟子、荀子代表儒家，老子、庄子代表道家，墨子代表墨家等等。他们的争论使中国的思想文化出现了"百家争鸣"的繁荣局面。

战国时期，秦国依靠商鞅变法，国家富强，后来灭掉六国，统一了中国。

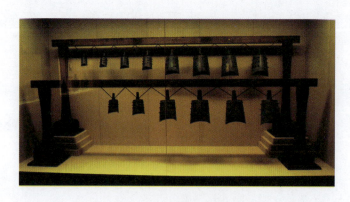

战国时期的编钟（古代乐器）

生词

zhī chí 支持	support		jiǎng lì 奖励	award
chēng bà 称霸	seek hegemony		gēng dì 耕（地）	cultivate
gǎi gé 改革	reform		pǔ biàn 普遍	universally
yāo qǐng 邀请	invite		yě liàn 冶（炼）	smelt
chéng dù 程度	degree		guī mó 规模	scale
xiào 孝	filial piety		liú tōng 流通	flow
fèi chú 废除	abolish		dòng dàng 动荡	turmoil
guān jué 官爵	official ranking		zhēng lùn 争论	dispute

听写

任用　废除　孝　奖励　普遍　支持　改革　争论

耕地　冶炼　*程度　邀请

比一比

持 { 支持 / 持久 / 主持 }　　解 { 解放 / 解开 / 了解 }　　争 { 争论 / 争夺 / 战争 }　　{ 废（废除） / 费（花费） }

程 { 程度 / 路程　　普 { 普遍 / 普通　　改 { 改革 / 改变　　冶 { 冶（冶炼）/ 治（治病）

字词运用

废除

我们已经废除了这些旧制度，建立了新制度。

废物

旧报纸是废物，但是还可以利用。

规模

上海造船厂的规模很大，有成千上万的工人。

规矩

开车要守规矩，不要超速。

支持

李青的意见得到了大多数人的支持。

回答问题

1. 春秋时期的特点是什么?

2. "战国七雄"指的是哪些国家?

3. 秦为什么会强盛起来?

4. 你听说过都江堰吗?

词语解释

一般——普通;通常。

任用——委派人担任职务。

度量衡——计量长短、容积、重量的统称。

封建社会——一种社会制度,特征是地主占有大量土地,农民没有或有很少的土地,只能耕种地主的土地。

争鸣——比喻在不同的思想或观点上进行争论。常用"百家争鸣"。

阅读

商鞅的故事

商鞅,战国时期政治家。他原是卫国人,后到秦国说服秦孝公变法强国。

商鞅认为追求名利是人的本性,提出"利出于地,名出于战",鼓励人们通过辛勤种地和勇敢作战来获得名利。公元前356年,秦孝公任用商鞅,开始变法。

商鞅在变法前,将一根长木头放在城的南门,并说谁能把木头搬到北门,赏十金。城门口围了许多老百姓看热闹,谁也不相信这是真的。商鞅看没人搬木头,就又说谁将木头搬到北门赏五十金。果然有一个人走出来,将木头搬到北门。商鞅马上赏给这人五十金,以此说明政府说话算数。这件事很快传遍了全国,老百姓都知道必须遵守变法的法令,秦国就开始改革了。

新法规定:在全国设立41个县,派官员管理。而官位、爵位要有军功才能得到;王亲贵族如

立木为信
(清《东周列国志》)

果没有军功就不能得到贵族身份。这样一来，秦兵同敌人作战都很勇敢，达到了强兵的目的。新法把国家的土地分给农民，土地属于私人，可以自由买卖。商鞅认为农业对发展经济很重要，所以新法规定，凡是生产粮食和布帛多的人，可以减免劳役和税，凡是因经商，不积极生产而贫困的，将全家充为官府奴婢。商鞅又统一了度量衡，便利了商业往来。新法一公布，秦国的旧贵族便出来反对，他们指使太子犯法，破坏新法推行。商鞅把带头反对新法的旧贵族杀了。旧贵族们十分痛恨商鞅，总想害他。有一次在酒席上，一个叫赵良的人看到商鞅很得意，就提醒他说："你的寿命像早上的露水一样，长不了。你还不如把封地还给国君，到边远的地方去种地吧。"商鞅没有理会他的意见。秦孝公死后，商鞅就被贵族杀害了，但是新法却一直在秦国执行。秦不断强大，最后统一了中国。

生词

míng lì 名利	fame and gains	láo yì 劳役	penal servitude
gǔ lì 鼓励	encourage	shuì 税	tax
fǎ lìng 法令	rule	nú bì 奴婢	slave or maid
shēn fen 身份	capacity; identity	tí xǐng 提醒	remind
jiǎn miǎn 减免	reduce	lǐ huì 理会	hear; adopt

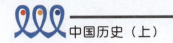

Lesson Three

The Spring and Autumn Period and the Warring States Period

The Eastern Zhou (about 770BC-256BC) lasts for more than five hundred years and it is usually divided into two periods: the Spring and Autumn Period (770 BC - 476 BC), and the Warring States Period (475 BC - 221 BC).

The main feature during the Spring and Autumn Period was large states seeking hegemony. At the beginning of the Spring and Autumn Period, there were more than 100 vassal states fighting with each other for lands and population. The Emperor of Zhou had little power and had to depend on the economic and political support of powerful vassals. The first vassal seeking hegemony was Qi Huangong. Qi was a large state in the east and Huangong appointed Guan Zhong as his Prime Minister to manage and reform domestic affairs. The state of Qi became powerful and in 651 BC, Huangong gathered other vassals and had himself elected as the leader of the alliance. Later on, the state of Jin led by Jin Wengong become the most powerful and the hegemony in the central plains at the middle and lower reaches of the Yellow River. Later on, more hegemony appeared, including Chu Zhuangwang, and Qin Mugong. Other states fighting for ruling power included Song in central plains as well as Wu and Yue located along the downstream reach of the Yangtze River.

In 475 BC, the Warring States Period began and only more than 20 states survived over 360 years of wars, among which the seven states of Qi, Chu, Yan, Han, Zhao, Wei, and Qin were the most powerful and they were known as Top Seven during the Warring States Period. The reason that these seven states were the most powerful was that they all carried out reforms to certain degrees, especially in the state of Qin. Qin Xiaogong supported Shang Yang to carry out reforms by abolishing hereditary system of official ranking and titular honors and by awarding those with meritorious military service. The traditional enfeoffment was abolished and the state was divided into 41 counties to be managed by the officials appointed by the emperor. The original nine-square system of land ownership (in ancient China with one large square divided into nine small ones, the eight outer ones being allocated to serfs who had to cultivate the central one for the serf owner) was abolished for the implementation of private land ownership so as to encourage cultivating and weaving. In addition, the weights and measures were also unified throughout the state. Although Shang Yang was later killed by the noblemen, yet the reforms he advocated were carried on and laid a solid foundation for the final unification achieved by Qin.

During the Warring States Period, through effective reforming measures, the land could be sold and bought freely, which greatly stimulated the production enthusiasm of the peasants. The iron agricultural tools had been universally adopted and a great many of water conservancy projects had been constructed

including the irrigation of farm lands by channeling the water of the Zhang River in the state of Wei and the construction of Dujiang Dam and Zhengguo Dyke by the state of Qin, which promoted the rapid development of agriculture at the time. As for handicraft industry, the iron smelting, the production of lacquer wares and the construction of boats achieved large scale and reached high technical level. While at the same time, the urban population increased and there were considerable currency flows, making businessmen an important social force at the time. Since then, China had been a feudal society.

During the Spring and Autumn Period and the Warring States Period, there were never ending wars and great social turmoil and changes. While at the same time, this was also a period with flourishing ideologies and cultural development. Philosophers proposed different theories and thoughts including among which the Confucian school advocated by Confucius, Mencius and Xunzi, the Taoist school advocated by Laozi and Zhuangzi, as well as the Mohist School with Mozi as representative. Their disputes reflected the cultural development and ideological liberation at the time.

During the Warring States Period, the state of Qin became prosperous and powerful thanks to the reforms conducted by Shang Yang. Later on, Qin destroyed other six major states one by one and finally unified the entire China.

Stories about Shang Yang

Shang Yang was a statesman during the Warring States Period. He was originally the resident of the state of Wei and went to the state of Qin to persuade Qin Xiaogong to promote the state with reforms.

Shang Yang believed that it was human nature to seek fame and gains; therefore, he proposed that people could get gains through farming and could achieve fame through fighting. People were thus encouraged to work hard in farmland and to fight bravely in battlefield. In 356 BC, Qin Xiaogong appointed Shang Yang and supported his reform policies.

Before starting his reforms, Shang Yang ordered to put a long log at the south entrance of the city and promised ten *jin* gold to the one who moved the log to the north entrance of the city. A large crowd gathered at the entrance but nobody believed that it was true. Shang Yang saw that no one moved the log and then raised the award to fifty *jin* gold. Then a man stepped out and moved the log to the north entrance. Shang Yang awarded the man with fifty *jin* gold immediately and showed with fact that the government would keep the promises. This event was soon spread over the whole country, and all the people realized that they must obey the laws of reform. After this, the reforms started in the state of Qin immediately.

According to the new rules, there were 41 counties in the state managed by the officials appointed by the emperor. Both the official rankings and titular honors were awarded to those with military exploits; no member of royal family and nobleman could get the titular noble honors without military merits. Accordingly, the soldiers all fought bravely with enemies and the combat power was greatly improved. According to the new rules, the state land was allocated to peasants and the privately owned land could be traded freely. Shang Yang held that agriculture was important for the development of economy, therefore the new rules made it clear that those producing more grains and silk could have their penal servitude and taxes reduced. The entire family of a businessman becoming poverty-stricken due to laziness would be either slaves or maids serving local authorities. Shang Yang later unified weights and measures and facilitated transactions. At the publishing of new rules, the traditional noblemen of the state stood up against it. They then abetted the crown prince to break law so as to prevent the implementation of new rules. Shang Yang ordered to kill the old noblemen leaders against the new rules; therefore they hated him so much that they wanted him to die. Once a man named Zhao Liang said to Shang Yang: "Your life is like the dew in early morning and cannot last long. Why don't you return your fief to his majesty and go to remote place farming?" Shang Yang was not frightened and insisted on his reform. Later on, Qin Xiaogong died and Shang Yang was killed by noblemen. But the reforms were carried on continuously and the state of Qin became increasingly powerful until it unified the entire China.

第四课

秦

公元前221年秦王嬴(yíng)政建立了中国历史上第一个统一的封建帝国。他自称"始皇帝",也就是秦始皇。

秦朝(前221年—前206年)废除了分封制,实行郡县制:在首都咸阳设立朝廷,把全国分为36郡,郡下有县,县下还有乡和亭。皇帝权力至高无上,无论朝廷还是地方的各级官员都由他任命。这一套完整的政治制度在中国基本上沿用了两千多年。

秦始皇画像

公元前216年,秦始皇下令全国申报田产,按亩纳税,从法律上承认土地私有;同时,废除六国旧货币,推行统一的新货币;废除六国旧度量衡,实行统一的度量衡。秦始皇时,还统一了全国的文字、道路的宽度

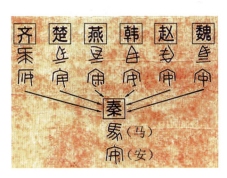

秦统一文字

和车辆车轮间的距离。这在当时称为"书同文，车同轨"。

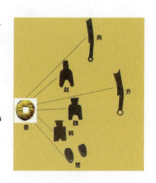

秦统一货币

为巩固政权，秦始皇大修道路，巡游各地。他又叫人烧毁六国史书，禁止私人收藏儒家书籍；还逮捕了460多个读书人，在咸阳坑杀。

为了征服百越地区①，秦始皇派军队进入岭南，并命人开凿灵渠，沟通了长江和珠江两大水系；同时又派大将蒙(méng)恬(tián)北击匈奴，收回河南（现今河套及以南）地区。他还动用大批劳力修补并连接了秦、赵、燕(yān)原有的长城，这就是著名的万里长城。

秦统一中国后，每年都要用300万的成年男子（当时全国人口约为2,000万）修建各项工程，包括秦始皇庞大的宫殿和陵

金山岭万里长城

---

① 百越地区——古代指中国广东、广西一带的地区。

墓,再加上重税、刑罚,农民们实在活不下去,被迫起来反抗。公元前209年陈胜、吴广在大泽乡(今安徽宿(sù)州市)起义。起义军快打到咸阳时,被秦军击败,吴广被部下谋害,陈胜被他的车夫杀死。这时各国旧贵族也纷纷起兵。其中一位义军将领项羽在巨鹿大破秦军主力。另一位义军将领刘邦带兵攻下咸阳。秦灭亡。

秦灭亡以后,项羽兵力强大,自立为西楚霸王并封刘邦为汉王。后来,由于刘邦善于用人,深得民心,最后打败了项羽,项羽退到乌江边自杀。

生词

jùn xiàn 郡县	prefectures and counties	guǐ dào 轨(道)	rail
cháotíng 朝廷	court	gǒng gù 巩固	solidify
tíng 亭	inn (administrative institution in Qin Dynasty); pavillon	xún yóu 巡游	itinerate; travel
		dǎi bǔ 逮捕	arrest
shēn bào 申报	register	zhēng fú 征服	conquer; control
nà shuì 纳税	pay tax	xíng fá 刑罚	penalty; punishment
fǎ lù 法律	law	móu hài 谋害	murder
huò bì 货币	currency	xiàng 项	Xiang (surname); measure word

听写

法律　申报　纳税　轨道　亭　货币　刑罚　项　巩固

巡游　*逮捕　征服

比一比

轨 { 轨道 / 铁轨 }　　捕 { 逮捕 / 捕鱼 }　　{ 亭（亭子）/ 停（停止）}　　{ 巩（巩固）/ 筑（建筑）}

货 { 货币 / 货物 }　　游 { 巡游 / 旅游 }　　{ 廷（朝廷）/ 庭（家庭）}　　{ 项（项目）/ 顶（山顶）}

字词运用

申报

过海关时旅客要申报所带的贵重物品。

伸出

中医治病时经常要求病人伸出舌头来看一看。

轨道

地球沿着一定的轨道围绕太阳转动。

铁轨

火车在铁轨上运行。

回答问题

1. 秦帝国是由谁在哪一年建立的？

2. 秦是不是中国历史上第一个统一的封建帝国？

3. 秦始皇推行了哪些政策？

4. 文字的统一对中国历史的发展有什么样的影响？

5. 谈谈你所知道的万里长城。

6. 你听说过灵渠吗？

7. 秦末农民起义的原因是什么？领导人是谁？

词语解释

郡县——古代的行政区划。

至高无上——最高，没有更高的。

长 城

在秦统一六国前，匈奴人经常侵入内地掠夺牛羊、粮食，使相邻的燕、赵、秦国深受其害。尤其是秦灭六国时，匈奴乘机占领了河套地区。秦朝建立后，派大将蒙恬带30万大军攻打匈奴，收回河套南北的广大地区，并在这里设立郡县。为了留住这片土地，秦始皇又动用30万民工，让他们在北方的风雪中，肩挑手抬，花费了十多年的时间，将秦、赵、燕旧时长城连接起来，重新加固。民工们留下无数的白骨，终于建成了举世闻名的万里长城。

长 城

阿房宫

秦灭六国时，每灭一国，就命人画下这个国家宫殿的图样，在咸阳仿造。全国统一后，秦始皇兴修的宫殿中规模最大的是阿房宫。阿房宫究竟有多大，后人是难以想象的。据说，阿房宫的前殿东西长500步，南北长50丈，里面可坐一万人。殿门以磁石做成，以防有人暗藏铁兵器入宫行刺。殿门前排列着12个铜人。

它们是用从民间没收的武器铸成的。这个浩大的工程前后使用了七八十万人，不过，还没有等到它建成，秦始皇就死了。后来项羽攻占咸阳后放火焚烧，大火一连烧了三个月都没有熄灭。

2002年中国考古学家开始发掘阿房宫遗址。考古报告说阿房宫前殿遗址的台基东西长1,270米，南北宽426米，但没有发现它被大火烧过的痕迹。目前，考古工作还在进行，阿房宫的秘密还没有被揭开。

灵 渠

秦始皇派出50万大军南下，为了运粮运兵，派人在今广西兴安开凿运河，这就是著名的灵渠。渠全长34千米，沟通了长江水系和珠江水系。因为渠的构思巧妙，所以起名"灵渠"。灵渠的修成对中原地区和西南的经济文化交流起了重要作用。

焚书坑儒

秦朝建立初期，秦始皇为了巩固他的统治下令"焚书"。除了国家收藏外，民间收藏的《诗经》、《尚书》、诸子百家的著作都必须交出烧掉，只留秦国史书、医药、占卜、种植之类的书籍。后来，秦始皇又将

兵马俑（秦）

400多个反对他的读书人活埋。史称"焚书坑儒"。秦始皇想以这种方式来统一思想文化，但却造成中国文化遗产的重大损失。

生词

qīn rù 侵入	invade	mò shōu 没收	confiscate; take possession of
lüè duó 掠夺	plunder; seize	fén shāo 焚烧	burn
méng tián 蒙恬	Meng Tian (name)	tái jī 台基	base of a structure above ground
ē páng gōng 阿房宫	The Epang Palace	gòu sī 构思	design
fǎng zào 仿造	copy; model on	yí chǎn 遗产	heritage
xíng cì 行刺	assassinate		

译文 English Translation

Lesson Four

Qin

Emperor Yingzheng founded the first consolidated feudal empire in the history of China in 221BC and entitled himself Emperor Shi (the first emperor) and was later known as Qin Shihuang (the first emperor of the Qin Dynasty).

During the Qin Dynasty (221-206BC), the enfeoffment was abolished and replaced by the system of prefectures and counties. The capital city at the time was Xianyang and the entire nation was divided into 36 prefectures. The counties were under the control of prefectures and the counties in turn managed villages and inn. The emperor was the sovereign of the nation and appointed officials of different levels to be in charge of different sectors. The complete political system lasted more than two thousand years.

In 216BC, Qin Shihuang ordered to register all the cultivated farmland throughout the country and the land owners should pay tax according to the actual area of the land they owned. The private ownership of farmland was then legalized. At the same time, the old currencies originally used by the six states were replaced by newly issued currency; the old weights and measures used by the six states were replaced by unified ones. Under the reign of Qin Shihuang, a universal characters, unified road width and carriage rail had been adopted throughout the country, which was called "the same language, the same rail" at that time.

In order to solidify his political power, Qin Shihuang constructed a large number of roads and traveled all around the country. He ordered to burn the books recording the histories of six states and prohibited private collection of Confucian books. He ordered to arrest and burry over 460 Confucian scholars alive in Xianyang.

In order to control the area of Baiyue, Qin Shihuang sent army to South China and ordered to construct Lingqu canal so as to link two water systems of the Yangtze River and the Pearl River. He sent his favorite general Meng Tian to fight back the Hsiung-Nu in the north and recover the Henan area (today's Hetao and area to its south). Then he ordered to recruit a large amount of labors to mend and connect the defending walls of the Qin, Zhao and Yan to construct the world famous Great Wall.

After Qin unified China, the government drafted three million adult males (the total population at the time was 20 million) each year to construct various kinds of projects including his tremendous palace and mausoleum. This, together with heavy taxation and strict penalties, forced peasants to rise up against the government. In 209 BC, Chen Sheng and Wu Guang rose up in Dazexiang Village (today's Suzhou, Anhui Province). They fought their way close to the capital city of Xianyang and were defeated by the Qin army. Wu Guang was killed by his followers and Chen Sheng was killed by his cart-driver. At that time, the former noblemen of other states also raise troops against Qin. General Xiang Yu defeated the main force of Qin in Julu and another general Liu Bang led his men taking Xianyang and ended the reign of Qin.

After the collapse of Qin, Xiang Yu commanding the most powerful army crowned himself as the King of Western Chu and then conferred Liu Bang as the Prince of Han. Later on, since Liu Bang won high reputation among people, he finally defeated Xiang Yu, who ran away to the shore of the Wujiang River and committed suicide there.

The Great Wall

Before Qin merged six states, Hunnish people had always invaded the inland and plundered flocks, herds, and food supplies, causing a lot of losses to Yan, Zhao and Qin. When Qin fought with the armies of six states, the Hunnish people took the chance and occupied the area around the Great Bend of the Yellow River. After the unification of the state, Qin sent General Meng Tian with 300,000 soldiers to fight with the Hunnish people, recovered the area taken by them and established prefecture and counties there. In order to better control the area, Qin Shihuang ordered to recruit 300,000 laborers to constructing a defending project by joining the old walls originally built by Qin, Zhao, and Yan. After ten years of hard work at a price of tens of thousand lives, they accomplished the now world famous Great Wall.

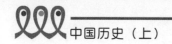

The Epang Palace

When Qin fought with six states, at destroying one state, the emperor would order to draw the royal palace for constructing the same one in Xianyang. After unifying China, Qin Shihuang built a lot of palaces and the largest one among them was the Epang Palace. It is hard to imagine how big the palace was. It is said that the distance from the east to the west of its front hall was 500 paces and that from the south to the north was 50 *zhang*, and the hall was big enough for ten thousand people sitting inside it. The doors of the hall were made of magnet for fear of assassinators bringing weapons into the hall. In front of the hall, there were 12 copper statues made of the weapons confiscated from the civilians. The Epang Palace was a large-scale project and the annual number of laborers was nearly 800,000. Yet it was never accomplished, for after Qin Shihuang died, it was burnt at the order of Xiang Yu. The fire burnt on for three months.

In 2002, Chinese archaeologists started to excavated and investigated the site of Epang Palace. According to the exploration, the foundation basis of its front hall is 1,270 meters long from east to west and 426 meters wide from north to south; there is no sign indicating that the hall was burned. Currently, the archaeological work is still ongoing and the secret of Epang Palace hasn't been revealed yet.

The Lingqu Canal

Qin Shihuang sent 500,000 soldiers to the south and ordered to construct a canal in today's Xing'an of Guangxi Province to transport both food suppliers and armies. This was the well-known Lingqu Canal. Its total length was 34 kilometers linking two water systems of the Yangtze River and the Pearl River. The canal had been cleverly designed and hence its name, which meant the Clever Canal literarily. The construction of the canal was important to the economical and cultural communication between the area of the middle and lower reaches of the Yellow River and southwestern China.

Burning Books and Burying Confucian Scholars Alive

At the early period of Qin Dynasty, in order to consolidate his control over the entire country, Qin Shihuang ordered to burn books. Apart from national collections, the privately collected *Books of Odes*, *Books of History* and the works of more than one hundred schools should all be handed out and be burnt. Only the books on history of Qin state, medical sciences, divination and planting could be kept. Later on, he ordered to bury more than 400 Confucian scholars alive. These are known as "Burning Books and Burying Confucian Scholars alive" in Chinese history. Qin Shihuang wanted to unify the thoughts and culture by these means, but it caused great losses to Chinese cultural heritage.

第五课

西 汉

公元前206年，刘邦建立汉王朝，定都长安（今西安），史称西汉。刘邦接受了秦灭亡的教训，决定让百姓休养生息，办法是让士兵复员，让逃亡农民返回家乡，释放奴隶，奖励农耕，减轻田租等。西汉沿用秦的政治制度，减轻刑罚，安定社会。

经过几十年的恢复和发展，到汉武帝时，西汉强盛起来。武帝又进一步削弱了汉初以来所封诸侯王的势力；以五铢钱为唯一通行全国的货币；又实行盐铁专卖；打击不法商人，增加国家财政收入；在军事上，建立了国家常备军队；在思想上，罢黜(chù)百家，独尊儒术。

汉武帝像

汉武帝时，中国出了一位著名的历史学家司马迁。他前后花了18年的时间，写出了中国第一部纪传体①通史——《史记》。《史记》全书共有本纪②、列传等130多篇，52万多字，叙述了从黄帝到汉武帝前后3,000多年的历史，记载了许多历史人物和历史事件。《史记》不仅是一部史书，而且还是一部优秀的文学作品，对后世影响极大。

西汉时，牛耕和铁制农具使用更普遍，铁犁上安有犁壁，用于翻碎土块。这比西欧早1,000年左右。耕作技术也有了很大改进。当时手工冶铁已能做到高温冶炼。纺织业更是发达，长沙马王堆汉墓出土的一件素纱单衣，又轻又薄，重量只有48克。汉代开通了历史上有名的国际贸易路线——"丝绸之路"。从长安出发，沿"丝绸之路"经过今天的河西走廊和新疆，可以到达中亚和西亚，甚至远到欧洲。当时商业和贸易繁荣、发达，城市规模扩大，大城市

西汉素纱单衣（长沙马王堆出土）

---

① 纪传体——中国传统史书的一种体裁，主要以人物传记为中心叙述史实。
② 本纪——纪传体史书中帝王的传记，按时间顺序记事，放在史书的最前面。

居民有几十万人，市场上各种商品琳琅满目。

西汉时，统一的多民族国家得到很大发展。汉朝与北方的匈奴之间既有战争，也有友好交往。汉武帝派张骞(qiān)出使西域（玉门关以西至中亚地区）以后，汉逐步控制了今天巴尔喀什湖以东和以南的广大地区。此外，又把南越（包括今天越南的北部、中部）纳入了版图。

汉并天下 瓦当

西汉中后期，土地集中到少数大地主手中，许多农民破产，沦为奴婢(bì)的人越来越多，加上政治腐败，就爆发了赤眉、绿林农民起义。义军占领长安，后来被刘秀（汉朝皇室后裔）打败。公元25年，刘秀登上王位，以今天的洛阳为国都，历史上称为东汉。

张骞出使西域路线图

生词

shì fàng 释放	release; set free	jū mín 居民	resident
tián zū 田租	land tax	lín láng mǎn mù 琳琅满目	full of beautiful things in eyes
huī fù 恢复	recovery	bā ěr kā shí 巴尔喀什	Barkashi
xuē ruò 削弱	cut down	bǎn tú 版图	territory
wǔ zhū qián 五铢钱	Five-zhu Currency	pò chǎn 破产	go bankrupt
zhuān mài 专卖	monopoly	fǔ bài 腐败	corrupt
dǎ jī 打击	crack down	zhàn lǐng 占领	capture
guó jì mào yì 国际贸易	international trade	hòu yì 后裔	descendent
zǒu láng 走廊	corridor		

听写

田租　打击　走廊　居民　破产　占领　恢复

琳琅满目　释放　*后裔

比一比

击 { 打击 / 袭击 }　　释 { 释放 / 解释 }　　削（削弱）/ 消（消灭）　　廊（走廊）/ 郎（女郎）

专 { 专卖 / 专家 }　　裔 { 后裔 / 华裔 }　　{ 版（版图）/ 板（黑板）}　　{ 租（田租）/ 组（小组）}

字词运用

恢复

范佳佳前一段时间生病住院，现在已经恢复健康，出院了。

腐败

汉朝末年政治腐败，危机重重。

腐烂

不能吃腐烂的水果。

反义词

削弱——增强　　　　　　　　减轻——加重

多音字

传 zhuàn

传 zhuàn { 列传 / 自传 }

传 chuán

传 chuán { 传说 / 传统 }

回答问题

1. 西汉王朝是由谁在哪一年建立的?

2. 西汉时，农民使用铁制农具是否很普遍?

3. 世界历史上有名的"丝绸之路"是哪个朝代开通的?

4. 请讲一讲你知道的"丝绸之路"。

词语解释

休养生息——让社会安定、人民休息，使人口繁殖。常指恢复并发展国家或人民的经济力量。

复员——因服务到期或战争结束，军人退出军队成为平民。

罢黜百家，独尊儒术——汉武帝时，只尊儒家思想，而排斥(chì)贬(biǎn)低其他各家学说。

琳琅满目——琳琅指美玉，比喻美好的东西很多。

纳入——放进；归入。

版图——指国家的疆域。

奴婢——男女仆人。

张骞通西域

张骞，西汉人。公元前139年，汉武帝派他出使西域。那时的西域指玉门关以西，至中亚、南亚和西亚一带。当时西域有36国，都受匈奴的欺负，他们渴望脱离匈奴。张骞和甘父等人离开长安向西走。可是没走多远就被匈奴抓住。匈奴王把张骞扣留下来。一转眼，十多年过去了，张骞已在匈奴娶妻生子，但是他仍然没有忘记他的使命。后来他逃出匈奴，终于找到大月氏。张骞劝说大月氏与汉朝共同攻打匈奴，但是大月氏不愿意。张骞这次出使虽然没有达到联合大月氏的目的，但是这13年，他掌握了西域的地理情况和风土人情。

公元前119年，张骞第二次出使西域，这次他带了300多人，还带了600匹马，牛羊万头，以及丝帛等大批礼物。由于河西走廊已经打通，路上很顺利。张骞不仅到达乌孙国，还派副使去大宛、大月氏、大夏、安息等国。公元前115年，张骞返回长安，乌孙国派出的使臣带着礼物也随他一同前来。他们看到汉朝地广人众，国家富强，回去以后报告了乌孙王，于是乌孙与汉朝和亲。张骞这次出使，使汉朝同西域各国建立了联系，各国使臣也纷纷前来汉朝。

张骞两次出使西域，使中国人发现了一个新世界，也加强了汉朝与西域各国的联系。他开辟的通往西域的道路，即"丝绸之路"，从西汉到唐一直是东西方贸易的要道。"丝绸之路"的开通大大促进了欧、亚、非各国与中国的友好往来和经济、文化交流，并对中国形成统一的多民族国家也产生了深远的影响。

生词

kě wàng 渴望	aspire to	dà ròu zhī 大月氏	Darouzhi (state)
tuō lí 脱离	break away	fù shǐ 副使	assisstant diplomatic envoy
kòu liú 扣留	detain	dà yuān 大宛	Dayuan (state)
shǐ mìng 使命	mission		

Lesson Five

The Western Han Dynasty

In 206BC, Liu Bang started the Han Dynasty. He chose Chang'an (today's Xi'an) as the capital city and this is known in the history as the Western Han Dynasty. Liu Bang learned lessons from Qin and allowed people to rehabilitate. He dismissed the army, encouraged fugitive farmers to return home, released slaves and maids, awarded those farming and reduced the rent. In addition, he adopted the political system of the Qin, eased penalties and tried to stabilize the society.

After dozens of years of recovery, the Western Han became prosperous powerful under the reign of Han Wudi. Wudi further restricted the power of the state conferred at the beginning of the Han Dynasty and unified different currencies with wu-zhu-qian (five-zhu currency). He monopolized salt and iron, cracked down unlawful businessmen and increased the financial revenue of the central government. In military field, he founded a regular central army; in the field of ideology, he rejected the various schools of thinkers and respected Confucianism only.

During the reign of Han Wudi, there was a famous historian named Sima Qian, who spent a total of 18 years in writing *Shi Ji* (Historical Records), the first general history of China in the style of Ji-zhuan-ti (the style emphasized the individuals and their performances). The book includes more than 130 pieces of *Benji* (biographies of emperors), *Liezhuan* (biographies of great figures) and so on, with a total of over 520,000 words, recording 3,000 years of history starting from Emperor Huang to Han Wudi and a large amount of historic figures and events. *Historical Records* is not only a history book but also an excellent literary work which has great influence on later generations.

During the Western Han Dynasty, farm cattle and iron agricultural tools were universally used. The iron plow was equipped with turn furrow to break the clod into pieces. The technique is about 1,000 years earlier than that in Western Europe. The farming techniques was greatly improved and iron smelting was processed by hand in high temperature. The cottoncracy was highly developed and a silk blouse excavated from the Han Tomb at Mawangdui of Changsha was extremely thin and light, weighing 48 grams only. During this period a famous international trade route, the Silk Road, was developed. It started from Chang'an and passed along today's Hexi Corridor and Xinjiang, reaching the Middle and West Asia or even as far as Europe. The business and trade at the time was prosperous and developed, the size of cities expanded with hundreds of thousands of residents living in big cities with a superb collection of beautiful things in market.

During the Western Han Dynasty, the unified multinational country expanded gradually. The Han nationality fought with northern nations including Hsiung-Nu; but there was also friendly exchange between them. Han Wudi sent Zhang Qian on a diplomatic mission to the Western Regions (west area of

Yumen Pass and the Central Asian areas) and then gradually controlled a vast area to the east and south of Barkashi Lake. Later, Nanyue (north and middle Vietnam today) was also become part of his territory.

During the middle and later periods of the Western Han Dynasty, the land resource was gathered once again in the hand of a few landlords and many peasants became slaves and maids. These, together with the element of political corruption, resulted in the breaking out of Chimei (red eyebrows) and Lulin peasant uprisings. The peasant soldiers captured Chang'an but were soon defeated by Liu Xiu (the descendent of the royal family of the Han Dynasty). In 25AD, Liu Xiu came to the throne and established today's Luoyang as the capital city. This was known as the Eastern Han Dynasty in the history.

Zhang Qian on Diplomatic Missions to the Western Regions

Zhang Qian was born during the Western Han Dyansty. In 139BC, Han Wudi sent him on his first diplomatic mission to the Western Regions. The Western Regions at that time referred to the areas to the west of Yumen Pass till the areas of Central Asia, South Asia and West Asia. There were 36 states in the Western Regions and all of them were bullied by Hsiung-Nu; therefore, they wanted to get rid of the control of Hsiung-Nu. Zhang Qian and Gan Fu led the team leaving Chang'an and heading toward the west. But they were soon captured by Hsiung-Nu and the king detained Zhang Qian. Ten years flied by, Zhang Qian married and had children in Hsiung-Nu. But he still remembered his mission. Later on, he fled away from Hsiung-Nu and finally found Darouzhi. Zhang Qian persuaded Darouzhi to fight with Hsiung-Nu together with Han but was refused. Although Zhang Qian failed in his first mission, yet during the thirteen years, he became familiar with the geography and customs of the Western Regions.

In 119 BC, Zhang Qian went to the Western Regions on his second mission. This time, he brought along 300 men, 600 horses, ten thousand flocks and herds as well as a large amount of presents including silk. Since the Hexi Corridor had been cleared, they had a smooth journey and went to the state of Wusun directly. At the same time, Zhang Qian sent assistant diplomatic envoys to other states of Dayuan, Darouzhi, Daxia and Anxi. In 115 BC, Zhang Qian returned to Chang'an with the envoys and presents sent by the state of Wusun. The envoys witnessed and reported to their king about the vast territory, prosperous society and powerful state of Han. The king then proposed marriage with the daughter of the Han imperial family. This time on his diplomatic mission, Zhang Qian helped the Han government in establishing diplomatic relations with many states in the area and accordingly, these states sent their envoys to Han Government.

Zhang Qian went to the Western Regions twice, helped Chinese find a new world outside and reinforce the relationship between Han Empire with the states in the West Region. The trade route he developed was later known as the Silk Road and became the main route for international trade from the Western Han Dynasty to Tang Dynasty, greatly promoting the friendly communications and exchanges between China and other countries in Europe, Asia and Africa. It also has a profound influence on the formation of a unified multinational state in China.

第六课

东 汉

"五星出东方"彩锦（新疆出土）

东汉王朝（公元25年—220年）是刘秀建立的。刘秀原是西汉王室的后代，统一全国后，他主张宽仁治国。他解放奴婢(bì)，减免租税，把公田分给或租给无地的农民，注意改进农具，发展生产。

东汉时期铁制农具有了很大改进，又修建了许多沟渠和堤坝，农业生产得到了恢复和发展。手工业方面，丝织、麻织技术进步显著，尤其是造纸技术有了重大突破，蔡伦用树皮、麻头、破布等原料造纸，大大降低了成本，使纸成了一般人都可以使用的东西，大大方便了文化的传播和发展。

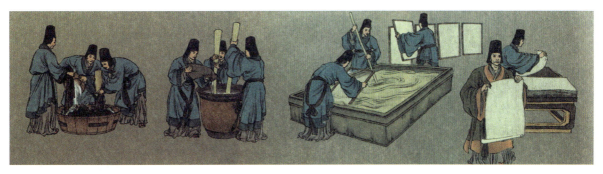

汉代造纸术

"医圣"张仲景

东汉时期科学技术取得了不少成就。天文学方面,张衡制造了浑天仪,反映星宿的运行。地震学方面,张衡还发明了地动仪,测定地震的发生和它的方位。医学方面出现了名医张仲景和华佗。东汉末年,天下大乱,传染病流行。张仲景虽然身为长沙太守,但是经常免费为病人治疗疾病,深受民众爱戴。经过数十年的努力,张仲景写出了中国第一部论述外感热病的专著《伤寒杂病论》。这部书是中国医学史上影响最大的一部古典医学著作,张仲景也被后人尊称为"医圣"。华佗则是一名杰出的外科医生,他发展了麻醉学和外科手术学。

汉代铁剪
(1958-1959
河南出土)

公元73年,为加强与周边少数民族的联系,汉朝又派班超出使西域。18年后,西域各国摆脱匈奴控制,重归东汉管辖。公元97年,班超还派甘英出使大秦(即罗马帝国)。甘英虽未到达目的地,但是已经到达了波斯湾。

家庭纺织图(东汉画像石)

东汉中期以后，社会危机日益严重。公元184年，张角兄弟组织了"太平道"，发动起义。他们用黄巾包头为标志，称"黄巾军"。坚持了九个月以后，起义失败了。在镇压黄巾军起义的过程中，全国各地出现了许多军阀，称雄一方，与朝廷对抗，东汉政权名存实亡。

生词

dī bà 堤坝	dyke	bǎi tuō 摆脱	break away
chuán bō 传播	communication	guǎn xiá 管辖	govern
dòng tài 动态	dynamics	mù dì dì 目的地	destination
zhāng zhòng jǐng 张仲景	Zhang zhongjing (name)	wēi jī 危机	crisis
huà tuó 华佗	Hua Tuo (name)	biāo zhì 标志	sign
chuán rǎn bìng 传染病	epidemics	jiān chí 坚持	insist on
miǎn fèi 免费	free of charge	zhèn yā 镇压	surpass
zhì liáo 治疗	treat	jūn fá 军阀	warlord
jí bìng 疾病	disease	zhèng quán 政权	regime
wài kē 外科	surgical		

听写

危机　免费　坚持　治疗　疾病　传染病　堤坝　标志

外科　目的地　*传播　政权

比一比

传 { 传染 / 传播 / 传说 / 传统 }　　政 { 政权 / 政治 / 政府 / 行政区 }　　持 { 坚持 / 支持 / 持久 / 主持 }　　{ 堤（堤坝）/ 题（习题）/ 提（提包）}

费 { 免费 / 花费 }　　危 { 危机 / 危险 }　　疗 { 医疗 / 治疗 }　　{ 播（传播）/ 翻（翻开）}

字词运用

杰出

张衡是汉代杰出的科学家。

成就

经过多年发展,各国的体育事业都取得了很大的成就。

传播

造纸术促进了文化的传播。

传染

妈妈感冒了,两天以后把我也传染上了。

回答问题

1. 东汉时期,中国在科学技术上有哪些成就?

2. 张衡是谁?他发明了什么?

3. 华佗是谁?他对医学有哪些贡献?

4. "医圣"是谁?他写了一部什么医学名著?

5. 蔡伦造纸是什么朝代的事情?

词语解释

显著——非常明显。

成就——事业上取得的成绩。

爱戴——敬爱并且拥护。

杰出——（才能、成就）出众。

称雄一方——靠着武力统治一块地方。

名存实亡——表面上还有，实际上已经不存在了。

对抗——对立；抵抗。

突破——指打破了原来的困难局面，进入一个新阶段。

阅读

外科神医华佗

华佗是东汉后期著名的医学专家、养生专家。他精通内科、外科、妇科、儿科、针灸科，尤其精于外科。他开创了"开腹"术。他先让病人用酒喝下"麻沸散"，等病人全身麻醉，没有知觉后，就开刀做手术。如果病在肠胃，就把肠胃切开，冲洗清除脏物，然后再缝合，上药，四五天后，伤口便能好起来；一个月

华佗像

之内，病人就会完全好了。医生做这种大手术，就是现在也不是一件容易的事。在世界医学史上，华佗在外科和麻醉学方面都有着重要的地位。

华佗还发明了一种叫"五禽戏"的锻炼身体的方法，大体上是模仿虎、鹿、熊、猿、鸟五种动物的动作，并把这些动作联结起来，编成一套健身体操。他的一个学生按照这个方法经常锻炼，结果活到了90多岁。

由于华佗医术高超，小说《三国演义》中就有一段华佗给关羽刮骨疗毒的故事。故事说：关羽打仗时被毒箭射中右臂。毒已渗入骨头。华佗听说后前来为关羽治病。他对关羽说："我怕你害怕，需要立一个柱子，柱子上吊一个环，把你的胳膊套入环中，用绳子捆紧，再盖住你的眼睛，然后我再给你开刀治疗。"关羽笑着说："不用捆。"关羽喝了几杯酒就与别人下起了棋，同时把胳膊伸给了华佗。华佗切开皮肉，用刀刮骨。在场的人吓得都用手捂着眼睛。再看关羽，他一边喝酒一边下棋。血流了一盆，骨头上的毒才刮完。关羽笑着对华佗说："我的胳膊现在曲伸自如，好像从前一样。华佗先生，你真是神医呀。"华佗也佩服关羽，说："我行医以来，从没见过像你这样勇敢的人，将军真是神人呀。"

虽然史书上记载给关羽治疗的医生并不是华佗，但是这则故事还是反映了人们对华佗医术的赞叹。

生词

kāi fù 开腹	celiotomy		mó fǎng 模仿	imitate
má fèi sǎn 麻沸散	Ma-fei-san (*drug*)		shèn rù 渗入	penetrate into
qín 禽	birds		gē bo 胳膊	arm
duàn liàn 锻炼	take exercise		wǔ 捂	cover

Lesson Six

The Eastern Han Dynasty

The Eastern Han Dynasty (25-220AD) was founded by Liu Xiu, a descendent of the Western Han imperial family. After unifying the nation, Liu Xiu advocated managing the state with leniency and beneficence. Therefore, he released slaves and maids, reduced rent and taxes, distributed or rented public farm land to peasants without land. He also emphasized the improvement of agricultural tools and development of production.

During the Eastern Han, the iron agricultural tools had been improved greatly; a lot of canals and dykes had been constructed. The agriculture were recovered and developed rapidly. As for the handicraft industry, the weaving techniques for silk and linen achieved outstanding progresses and important breakthrough had been made in making paper. Cai Lun used such materials as barks, hemp combings and rugs to make paper so as to reduce the cost and to make paper a common commodity that could be used by ordinary people, which facilitated the communication and popularization of culture.

Great achievements had also been achieved in scientific technologies during the Eastern Han Dynasty. As for astronomy, Zhang Heng produced the armillary sphere to reflect the movement of planets. And as for seismology, he invented seismoscope to measure earthquake happenning and its direction. In medical science, there were such famous doctors as Zhang Zhongjing and Hua Tuo. At the end of the Eastern Han Dynasty, epidemics broke out and Zhang Zhongjing serving as the prefect of Changsha treated patients free of charge and he was popular among local people. After dozens of years of efforts, he composed the first monograph on heat diseases caused by external factors in China, *Treatise on Febrile Disease*. This is the most influential classic medical book in the history of medical science in China and Zhang Zhongjing was therefore honored as Medical Saint by later generations. Hua Tuo was an excellent surgeon who developed anesthesiology and surgical operation.

In 73AD, in order to promote the relations with the surrounding ethnic minority, the Han government sent Ban Chao on a diplomatic mission to the Western Regions. Eighteen years later, the states of the Western Regions got rid of the control of Hsiung-Nu and pledged allegiance with the Eastern Han. In 97 AD, Ban Chao sent Gan Ying as envoy to Daqin (Roman Empire). Gan Ying never reached his destination, but he got as far as the Persian Gulf.

Since the middle of the Eastern Han Dynasty, social crisis became increasingly serious and in 184AD, Zhang Jiao and his brother organized the *Taipingdao* to initiate uprising. Since they all wore yellow headcloth, hence the name of Huangjin army. They fought for nine months and were then defeated. During the suppression of the uprising, a lot of warlords emerged and became local authorities against the central government. The regime of the Eastern Han actually existed in name only.

Hua Tuo the Highly Skilled Surgeon

Hua Tuo was a famous expert in medial sciences and in health preservation. He mastered internal medicine, surgery, gynecology, pediatrics, and acupuncture. He was especially famed for surgery. He was the first to do celiotomy. He would ask his patient to drink a drug named ma-fei-san. After the patient was under general anesthesia and lost consciousness, he would then begin to do operation. If the disease lied in the intestines and stomach, he would then cut it open, cleanse and remove the dirty things before stitching it and covering it with medicines. Four or five days later, the wound would heal up and the patient would recover within one month. It is not easy to do such operation even in today and the achievements Hua Tuo made in surgery and anesthesiology win him an important position in the history of world medical sciences.

Hua Tuo invented a physical exercise named Five Animal Game, imitating the action of five animals of tiger, deer, bear, ape, and bird and creating an exercise by joining these actions together. One of his students did the exercise and lived till 90 years old.

Due to his excellent skill, the novel *Romance of the Three Kingdoms* tells a story of Hua Tuo scraping away poison from the bone for Guan Yu: One day, during the fight, Guan Yu was shot in the right arm by a poisonous arrow and the poison penetrated into the bone. Hua Tuo heard about this and offered his treatment. He said to the general: "I'm afraid that you will be scared and therefore order to erect a pole and there is a loop suspended from it. I will have your arm into the loop and tied tight with rope. Then I'll cover your eyes before operation." Guan Yu laughed at his prudence: "I don't need rope." The general had a couple of drinks and then began to play chess with others while unfolding his arm to Hua Tuo. Hua Tuo cut through the skin and flesh, using a knife to scrape away poison from the bone. At the scene, other people were all so frightened that they covered their eyes with hands. But Guan Yu was still drinking and moving his pieces on chessboard. The blood filled one basin and the poison was finally removed from the bone. Guan Yu smiled at his doctor: "I can fold and extend my arm freely, just like before. It's no lie that they all praise you as a highly skilled surgeon." Hua Tuo said to him: "I've never seen a patient like you before since I practiced medicine. You are no ordinary man indeed."

According to historical book, it was not Hua Tuo who treated Guan Yu, yet the story shows that people highly praise the surgical skill of Hua Tuo.

第七课

三国鼎立

东汉末年,军阀混战。其中曹操和袁绍的势力最大。曹操是在镇压黄巾起义过程中起家的,他收编了黄巾军30多万人,加强了自己的军事力量。后来他又实行屯田制①,解决了缺少军粮的问题。公元196年,曹操把东汉最后一位皇帝汉献帝迎接到许都(今许昌),控制在自己手中,在政治上取得了有利地位。公元200年,曹

曹操

---

① 屯田制——有军屯和民屯两种:组织失地的流民在官员的管理下开荒种地,是民屯;军队官兵及家属组织起来种田的,是军屯。

操率军3万迎战袁绍的10万大军，在官渡（在今河南）以少胜多，打败袁绍，占领了袁绍的地盘，统一了中国北方。公元208年，曹操乘胜南下，想吞并江南，统一全国。当时，汉朝皇室后裔刘备占据夏口（今湖北汉口），他接受了军师诸葛亮的建议，与掌握江东六郡（长江以南地区）的孙权结盟，共同抗曹。曹兵约20万人，号称80万，与孙刘联军5万余人相遇于赤壁（在今湖北），联军用火攻，曹军大败，逃回北方。后来，曹操全力消灭北方各地的军阀，完成了北方的统一。公元220年曹操死，他的儿子曹丕(pī)废汉献帝自立为帝，国号魏，定都洛阳。赤壁之战以后，刘备控制了四川一带。公元221年，刘备于成都称帝，国号汉，史称蜀汉。孙权也在公元229年称帝，国号吴，都城建业（今南京）。至此，魏、蜀、吴三国鼎立局面形成。

曹操

曹魏在政治、经济方面都有些改进措施。曹操提出"唯才是举"，重用有才干的人；又命令各郡县实行屯田，还向屯田的农民发放贷款购买耕牛、农具和种子，

古代战船图

恢复和发展了农业生产。

诸葛亮

蜀国自刘备死后,由诸葛亮执政,政治稳定,经济也有一定发展。诸葛亮又联合吴国,平定南中(今四川南部及云南、贵州一带),五次北伐,想要夺取中原,但是没有成功。

由于吴国战乱较少,中原地区的人民大量南迁,吴的农业、手工业有所发展。当时制造的大海船能装载六七百人。

公元263年,魏攻打蜀,蜀王刘禅(shàn)投降,蜀汉灭亡。公元265年,司马炎废掉魏国最后一个皇帝,建立晋朝,史称西晋。公元279年,晋国攻打吴国,第二年,吴王投降。中国在经历了90年的战乱和分裂之后,又归统一。

三国故事(邮票)

第七课

生词

yuán shào 袁绍	Yuan Shao (*name*)	dài kuǎn 贷款	loan
shōu biān 收编	incorporate into one's own force	gòu mǎi 购买	purchase
tún tián 屯田	open up wasteland and grow food grain	zhí zhèng 执政	come into power
xǔ chāng 许昌	Xuchang (*place*)	zhàn luàn 战乱	war
jiàn yì 建议	suggestion	zhuāng zài 装载	contain
jú miàn 局面	situation	tóu xiáng 投降	surrender
gǎi jìn 改进	improve	fēn liè 分裂	separation
cuò shī 措施	measure		

听写

建议　许昌　稳定　改进　投降　局面　分裂　统一

购买　袁　*贷款

比一比

建 { 建议 / 建立 / 建筑 }　　措（措施）/ 错（错误）　　袁（袁绍）/ 猿（猿人）　　屯（屯田）/ 吨（一吨）

编 { 收编 / 编织   贷 { 贷(贷款) / 货(货物)   { 昌(许昌) / 冒(冒烟)   { 执(执政) / 势(势力)

字词运用

建议

在计算机前工作了一天，妈妈建议我游游泳，放松一下。

建设

短短几年内，上海浦东(pǔ)就建设成了一个现代化的新区。

反义词

分裂——统一　　　　　　　　发放——收回

多音字

降(xiáng)　　　　　　　降(jiàng)

投降(xiáng)　　　　　　降(jiàng)落伞

zài   zǎi

载   载

zài   zǎi

装载   记载

回答问题

1. "三国"指哪三个国家？

2. 你知道三国时期的哪些历史人物？

3. 你听过"火烧赤壁"的故事吗？

词语解释

结盟——约定成为盟友。

称帝——当了皇帝。

措施——专门为解决某个问题采取的办法（用于较大的事情）。

火烧赤壁

曹操统一北方后，发展生产，增强了兵力。公元208年，曹操率大军20万南下，想消灭刘备和孙权。

当时刘备在湖北,只有2万兵马;孙权占江东六郡,有3万兵马。曹军南下,情况十分紧急。刘备的军师诸葛亮主张与孙权联合,共同抗击曹操。诸葛亮去见孙权,向孙权分析了两军的实力,认为孙刘联军一定可以打败曹军。孙刘联军屯兵长江南岸的赤壁,而对面长江北岸就是曹操的军队。一场大战就要开始了。

曹操虽然兵多,但是他的士兵多数是北方人,到了南方水土不服,常常生病;没生病的士兵也多晕船,加上不会游泳,这大大地削弱了曹军的战斗力。曹操十分着急,就采用了"连环船"的办法,将战船用铁链连在一起,然后再铺上木板,人在上面走就像在平地上走一样。

孙刘联军的统帅周瑜知道了曹操用"连环船"的办法,就与诸葛亮等人商量对策,决定让吴国大将黄盖假装投降曹操,用火

草船借箭(清代年画)

来烧曹军的连环船。曹操对黄盖要来投降信以为真，还跟他约定了来降的日期和暗号。到了那天，黄盖带领十艘小船向北岸划来，船上装满浇了油的干草和柴禾。等到了离曹营不远的地方，十只船上一齐放火。当时正刮东南风，火船像箭一样向曹军水寨驶去，把曹操的连环船烧着了。火越烧越大，很快就烧成一片火海。曹军乱作一团，士兵们有的落水而死，有的被烧死。孙刘联军又从水上和陆上猛攻曹军。曹军大败。曹操只好带着残兵败将逃回许都。自从赤壁兵败以后，曹操再也没有力量向南进军了。

生词

tún bīng 屯兵	station troops	pū 铺	lay
shuǐ tǔ bù fú 水土不服	be unaccustomed to the climate of a new place	rì qī 日期	date
		àn hào 暗号	secret signal
yùn chuán 晕船	become seasick	shǐ 驶	drive; sail
tiě liàn 铁链	iron chain	cán bīng bài jiàng 残兵败将	remnants of a defeated army

Lesson Seven

The Three Kingdoms of Wei, Shu Han and Wu

At the end of the Eastern Han, warlords engaged in the tangled warfare, Cao Cao and Yuan Shao were the most powerful among them. Cao Cao started to build up his power during the suppression of the Huangjin Uprising. He incorporated over 300,000 risers to greatly increase his military power. He also ordered his garrison troops and peasants to open up wasteland and grow food grain so as to gather enough army provisions. In 196AD, Cao Cao sent the last emperor of the Eastern Han Dynasty, Han Xiandi, to Xudu (today's Xuchang), for a convenient control and favorable political position. In 200AD, Cao Cao led 30,000 soldiers fighting and finally defeating 100,000 army led by Yuan Shao at Guandu (in today's Henan Province). Then Cao Cao marched toward the Hebei, captured the territory originally claimed by Yuan Shao and unified the North China. In 208AD, Cao Cao led his army heading toward the south for conquering the south and unifying the entire country. At that time, Liu Bei, the descendent of imperial family of Han, had retreated to Xiakou (today's Hankou in Hubei Province). He followed the suggestion of Zhuge Liang, his military counselor, and formed an alliance with Sun Quan, who guarded six prefectures to the south of the Yangtze River, to fight against Cao Cao. The 200,000 army led by Cao Cao was claimed to be 800,000 and fought with 50,000 allied forces of Sun and Liu at Chibi (in today's Hubei Province). The allied forces adopted the strategy of fire attack to defeat the enemies and forced Cao to return to the north. After the war at Chibi, Cao Cao focused on the management of the north and achieved unification in North China. In 220AD, Cao Cao died and his son Cao Pi ascended the throne by dethroning Han Xiandi. This was Wei and the capital city was Luoyang. After the war at Chibi, Liu Bei controlled the area in Sichuan and ascended the throne in 221AD. This was Han (Shu) and the capital city was Chengdu. Sun Quan ascended the throne in 229AD and this was Wu, the capital city was Jianye (today's Nanjing), hence the period of the Three Kindoms of Wei, Shu Han and Wu.

The kingdom of Wei adopted many measures in improving its politics and economy. Cao Cao proposed that the only criterion for selecting officials was talents. He put those with talents in very important positions and ordered to open up wasteland and grow food grain in all prefectures and counties. He also distributed land, farm cattle, agricultural tools and seeds to peasants.

As for the kingdom of Shu, after Liu Bei died, Zhuge Liang came into power. The kingdom maintained stable politically and achieved economic development. Zhuge Liang formed alliance with the kingdom of Wu, put down the rebellion in Southwest China (area of today's Yunnan and Guizhou Province, and southern area of today's Sichuan Province), organized five northern expedition aiming to capture central plains, but failed.

Since there were less wars in the kingdom of Wu, a large amount of people moved from the middle

and lower reaches of the Yellow River to the south, bringing along the development of both agriculture and handicraft industry in the area. The large sea boat built at that time could contain six to seven hundred people.

In 263AD, Wei attacked Shu and the surrender of Liu Shan marked the end of the kingdom of Shu Han. In 265AD, Sima Yan ascended the throne by dethroning the last emperor of Wei and founded Jin, which was known in the history as the Western Jin Dynasty. In 279AD, the Western Jin attacked the kingdom of Wu and the emperor of Wu surrendered on the second year. After a 90-year separation, China unified once again.

Fire Attack at Chibi

After Cao Cao unified the north China, he emphasized production and the improvement of military force. In 208AD, he led 200,000 soldiers heading toward the south to destroy the forces of Liu Bei and Sun Quan.

At that time Liu Bci was in Hubei with only 20,000 military forces, while Sun Quan occupied the six prefectures to the south of the Yangtze River with 30,000 soldiers. The approaching army of Cao Cao was extremely dangerous for both of them. Then Zhuge Liang suggested that Liu Bei formed alliance with Sun Quan to fight against Cao Cao together. Zhuge Liang went to visit Sun Quan and analyzed the actual strength of both sides, suggesting that an alliance would definitely defeat the army led by Cao. Then the allied forces of Sun and Liu guarded Chibi at the south bank of the Yangtze River, while the army of Cao was stationed at the north bank of the river. A great war was about to start.

The number of soldiers led by Cao Cao was multitudinous, but most of them were northerners and became sick for being unaccustomed to the climate of a new place; as for those who were not sick, most of them didn't swim. This greatly reduced the actual combat power of Cao's army and Cao Cao was worried about the situation. He then came up with the solution of joining all these warships together with iron chains, on which boards were laid for people to walk from one ship to another.

Zhou Yu was the commander in chief of the allied force of Sun and Liu. At realizing the strategy adopted by Cao Cao, he discussed with Zhuge Liang for countermove. They decided to let Huang Gai pretend to surrender to Cao Cao and then burn his warship connected together. Cao Cao believed in the surrender of Huang Gai and agreed on the specific date and secret signal. When the day came, the boats led by Huang Gai were full of hay and firewood. Huang Gai ordered to set their own boats on fire when coming near to the place where the enemy was stationed and the burning boats set fire on the warship of Cao that chained together. The strong eastern wind promoted the fire and turned the Cao barracks into a fire sea. The army led by Cao Cao fell into turmoil. Then the allied forces attacked in both the water and the land. Many soldiers of Cao Cao either burned to death or drowned. Cao Cao then led the survivors escape and back to Xudu. Since then, Cao Cao had never gathered enough force for a second expedition to the south.

第八课

两晋、南北朝

晋武帝司马炎建立西晋王朝后，恢复了分封制，封了同姓王国27个，其他小诸侯国500多个；政治上推行九品中正制①，使大贵族掌握了政权。西晋在经济上推行占田制，规定男子占田70亩，女子30亩，其中大部分土地要向国家纳税。

晋武帝死后，为争夺皇位，出现了"八王之乱"。宗室汝南王司马亮等八王互相混战16年，给国家和人民带来了无穷的灾难。西晋王朝的奢侈在中国历史上是少有的。有的官员一天的伙食费高达万钱；彼此为争胜斗富，竟用饴(yí)糖刷锅，用蜡当柴烧。各族人民生活非常困苦，不断爆发起义。当时，向黄河流域迁移的匈奴、氐(dī)、鲜卑等少数民族也纷纷起兵反晋，建立政权。公元311年，匈奴人攻破洛阳；五年后又攻破长安，西晋灭亡。

西晋灭亡以后，公元317年，宗室司马睿(ruì)在长江以南建立东

---

① 九品中正制——两晋南北朝时期一种选拔人才的制度。

晋政权，定都建康（今南京）。这时，由氐人建立的前秦政权已基本统一了中国北方。前秦皇帝苻(fú)坚自以为强大，十分骄傲，不听大臣的意见，一心想消灭东晋。公元383年，苻坚统率大军90万南下攻晋，东晋以8万兵迎击，战于淝(féi)水。结果苻坚大败，前秦瓦解，北方陷入分裂。战后，东晋得到了巩固。但在公元420年，东晋大将刘裕逼迫晋恭帝让位，自立为帝，建立了南朝第一个政权——宋；北方则被鲜卑拓跋(tuò bá)部建立的北魏政权统一。这是北朝的第一个政权。北魏在孝文帝时进行了改革，主要内容是实行均田制①以及使鲜卑族汉化。这一改革对社会经济的发展和各族人民的融合十分有益。

敦煌壁画

南方政权在宋之后，依次出现了齐、梁、陈政权的交替。北魏则又分裂。公元577年，北周统一中国北方。后来大臣杨坚废周帝自立，国号隋，建都长安。公元

---

① 均田制——北魏政权制定的一套农田分配制度，包括：国家给15岁以上男子分露田40亩，妇女20亩；所分露田不准买卖，死后归还政府等等。

《兰亭序》 王羲之

589年，隋军灭陈，统一全国。

两晋南北朝时期，由于社会动乱，战争连年，人民在痛苦中需要寻求安慰，因此佛教、道教流行。南朝皇帝甚至把佛教定为国教。也有人反对信教，如范缜写了《神灭论》，批驳佛教的因果报应、生死轮回、地狱天堂之说。在艺术方面，这一时期绘画和书法水平很高，画家顾恺之的名作《女史箴图》为传世珍品。东晋王羲之、王献之父子的书法成就尤其高，有"书圣"、"小圣"之称。在数学方面，南朝的祖冲之是世界上第一个把圆周率推算到小数点后7位数的人。地理学著作有郦道元写的《水经注》，农学著作有贾思勰写的《齐民要术》。

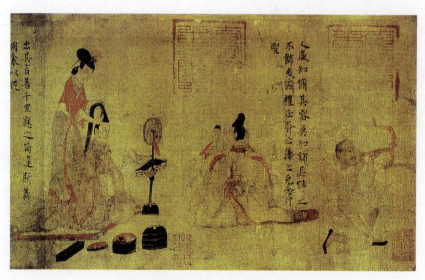

《女史箴图》局部（晋·顾恺之）

生词

rǔ nán wáng 汝南王	Runan King	xiàn rù 陷入	fall into
shē chǐ 奢侈	luxury	liú yù 刘裕	Liu Yu (*name*)
huǒ shí fèi 伙食费	money spent on meals	xiān bēi 鲜卑	Xianbei (*nationality*)
bǐ cǐ 彼此	each other	róng hé 融合	merge
là 蜡	wax	pī bó 批驳	refute
qiān yí 迁移	move	huì huà 绘画	painting
wǎ jiě 瓦解	disintegrate; break down	yuán zhōu lǜ 圆周率	pi (π)

听写

迁移　圆周率　陷入　绘画　瓦解　交替　蜡　安慰

伙食费　内容　*奢侈　融合

比一比

推 { 推行　推算　推翻 }　　融 { 融合　金融　融化 }　　动 { 动乱　动荡　运动 }　　流 { 流行　流动　河流 }

批 { 一批 / 批驳 }　　瓦 { 瓦解 / 瓦匠 }　　伙 { 伙食费 / 伙伴 }　　替 { 交替 / 代替 }

多音字

率 lǜ　　　率 shuài
圆周率 lǜ　　率领 shuài

回答问题

1. 两晋南北朝时期，为什么佛教、道教流行？

2. 顾恺之、王羲之、祖冲之分别在哪些方面取得了成就？

词语解释

宗室——皇帝同一父系家族的成员。

饴(yá)糖——用米和麦芽为原料制成的糖。

因果报应——佛教用语，指善有善报，恶有恶报，今生种什么因，来生结什么果。

生死轮回——佛教认为有生命的东西永远像车轮一样在天堂、地狱、人间等六个范围内循(xún)环转化。

小知识

云冈石窟

云冈石窟

云冈石窟位于山西省大同市，是北魏石窟艺术的代表，与敦煌的莫高窟、洛阳的龙门石窟并称为中国的三大佛教石窟艺术宝库。它依山开凿，东西长1,000米，雕刻着5万多尊大大小小的佛像。左图的佛像高达13.7米，是云冈石窟中最著名的。

阅读

木兰从军

北魏后期，生活在北方的柔然、契丹等少数民族逐渐强大起来。他们经常派兵到中原抢夺财物，掳走百姓。因此北魏朝廷常常大量征兵，派到边境去驻防。北魏民歌《木兰辞》所说的木兰替父从军的故事就发生在这个时期。据说木兰姓花，会纺织，还喜欢骑马、射箭，有一身好武艺。有一年，皇帝要征木兰的父亲去当兵。父亲已经年老，木兰没有哥哥，弟弟又小。怎么办呢？

木兰从军（杨柳青年画）

木兰坐在织布机旁发愁叹气。她想来想去，只有自己女扮男装替父从军。父母没有别的办法，只好同意了。北魏时候，从军作战，战马和武器都得由战士自己买。木兰买了马、马鞍和武器，女扮男装，告别父母姐弟，上路从军去了。木兰随军在黄河两岸作战。晚上宿营，她只能听到黄河哗哗的流水声和敌人骑兵战马的叫声，再也听不到父母亲切的呼唤。白天行军，木兰紧紧跟上，从不掉队；作战时，她冲杀在前，非常勇敢。木兰从军12年，立了不少战功。

战争结束了，皇帝要奖赏有功的将士，木兰既不想当官，也不想要钱，只想要一匹千里马，好赶快回家。木兰回到家乡，父母、弟弟、姐姐和邻居都来欢迎她。木兰回到自己的房间，换上女装，梳好头发，出门来见她的同伴。同伴们惊呆了。大家你看

木兰从军（邮票）

我，我看你，都说："木兰和我们一起打仗12年，我们竟然不知她是个女子。"

生词

róu rán 柔然	Rouran (nationality)		cóng jūn 从军	join the army
qì dān 契丹	Qidan (nationality)		wǔ yì 武艺	martial art
lǔ 掳	capture		zhēng bīng 征兵	enlist
zhù fáng 驻防	garrison		fā chóu 发愁	get worried

 English Translation

Lesson Eight

Two Jin Dynasties and the Northern and Southern Dynasties

After Jin Wudi, Sima Yan, founded the Western Jin Dynasty, he restored enfeoffment and conferred 27 kingdoms to Sima family and more than 500 small vassal states. He promoted nine-level administrative system in political field so as to guarantee that top noblemen held the political power. As in economic system, he advocated "land possession system" and regulated that men should be in possession of 70 *mu* farm land and women 30 *mu*, and that the owner should pay taxes for most land to the state.

After Jin Wudi died, eight princes including Runan King Sima Liang fought with each other for 16 years for the imperial throne, causing infinite disasters to both the country and its people. The luxury of the Western Jin Dynasty was unparalleled in the history of China. Some officials would spend ten thousand units of money on food each day; some would compete with each other in terms of wealth possession by using syrup to wash pan and using wax to burn as firewood. Since people were all poverty-stricken, there were always rebellious uprisings. The minorities including Hsiung-Nu, Di and Xianbei that had moved toward the area of the Yellow River also rose in revolt against Jin. In 311AD, Hsiung-Nu captured the city of Luoyang. Five years later, they took over Chang'an and marked the end of the Western Jin Dynasty.

After the collapse of the Western Jin and in 317AD, Sima Rui of the imperial family of Jin founded the Eastern Jin in Jiankang (today's Nanjing) and controlled the area to the south of the Yangtze River. At the same time, the Qianqin regime founded by the Di had almost unified the north China. Emperor Fu Jian of Qianqin was arrogant and believed that his state was powerful. In spite of the opposition of his officials, he determined to destroy the Eastern Jin. In 383AD Emperor Fu Jian of Qianqin led 900,000 soldiers heading the south and attacking Jin. The Eastern Jin gathered 80,000 soldiers to fight with Fu Jian at Feishui. Since most of the soldiers led by Fu Jian were not willing to fight and the emperor himself was so proud that he underestimated his enemies. He was then defeated and the north China fell apart. After the war, the Eastern Jin became more solidified. But in 420AD, General Liu Yu of the Eastern Jin overthrew Jin and founded Song, the first regime of the Southern Dynasty, while the north China was unified by the Northern Wei founded by Tuo Ba, a tribe of Xianbei. This is the first regime of the Northern Dynasty. Emperor Xiaowen of the Northern Wei carried out a reform to practice land-equalization system and to Chinesize the nationality of Xianbei. The reform effectively promoted social and economic development as well as the fusion of all nationalities.

As for the regimes in the south China, there was Qi, Liang, and Chen in turns after Song. Later the Northern Wei fell apart until Northern Zhou unified the northern China once again in 577AD. Later on, Minister Yang Jian ascended the throne by dethroning the emperor of Zhou and founded Sui in Chang'an. In 589AD, the army of Sui defeated Chen and unified the entire country.

During the Two Jin Dynasties and the Northern and Southern Dynasties, due to social turmoil and continuous wars, people desired to seek consolation to get rid of sufferings. Accordingly, Buddhism and Taoism prevailed. The emperors of the Southern Dynasty even ordered to take Buddhism as the national religion. But there were some against Buddhism; for example, Fan Zhen wrote his famous *On the Extermination of Deity* to criticize the cause and effect, wheel of life, hell and heaven advocated by Buddhism. In the field of art, painting and calligraphy had great achievements during this period of time. Gu Kaizhi the famous painter produced his masterpiece of *"Admonitions of the Instructress in the Palace"* that was to be handed down for generations as art treasure. Wang Xizhi the father and Wang Xianzhi the son of the Eastern Jin Dynasty had outstanding achievements in calligraphy and were famed as the "saint of calligraphy" and the "junior saint" respectively. In mathematics, Zu Chongzhi of the Southern Dynasty was the first in the world that calculated the "*pi*" and concluded accurately seven digits after the decimal point. In geography, Li Daoyuan produced *Shui Jing Zhu* (Commentary on the Waterways Classic); in agriculture, Jia Sixie wrote *Qi Min Yao Shu* (Important Arts for the People's Welfare).

Yungang Grottoes

Yungang Grottoes in Datong, Shanxi Province, represent the outstanding achievement of cave art during the Northern Wei. It is one of the top three treasuries of Buddhist cave art in China. The other two are Dunhuang Mogao Grottoes and Luoyang Longmen Grottoes respectively. The entire project was built on a mountain with a total length of 1,000 meters from east to west and over 50,000 Buddhist statuaries of different sizes. The statuary shown in the picture is 13.7 meters high and is a masterpiece of Yungang Grottoes.

Mulan Joined the Army

During the late period of the Northern Wei Dynasty, the minorities including Rouran and Qidan in the north became increasingly powerful and they always sent army to the middle and lower reaches of the Yellow River plundering property and capturing people. Accordingly, the government would always recruit soldiers to station in the border area. *The Ballad of Mulan*, a folk song of the Northern Wei Dynasty, told a story of Mulan replacing her father to join the army, which just happened during this period of time. It was said that Mulan was surnamed Hua and she knew how to weave, mastered horsemanship and archery, and was good at martial art. One year, Khan enlisted Mulan's father. But her father was old; she had no elder brother and her younger brother was too young. What could she do? Mulan sat beside her weaving machine and sighed. She thought it over and the only solution would be she disguised as a man and joined the army in place of her father. Her parents had no other choice but to agree on the plan. In the Northern Wei Dynasty, when a soldier joined the army, he had to buy war horse and weapon himself. Therefore, Mulan bought horse, saddle and weapon from the market, disguised herself as man, waved goodbye to her parents, her sister and brother, and was on her way to join the army. Mulan fought with enemies along the banks of the Yellow River along with her comrades in arms. When they camped out at the bank of the river, the only things that Mulan heard was the running water of the river and the whinny the horse rode by enemies. She could no longer hear the kind calls of her parents. In the days, Mulan would always follow the marching troops and never fell behind; during the war, she would be among the first to charge and fight bravely. During her 12 years of being a soldier, Mulan had achieved a lot of military exploits.

The war ended and the emperor wanted to reward the meritorious generals and soldiers. Mulan didn't want official ranking or money, the only thing she asked for was a horse that could travel one thousand *li* a day so that she could go back home sooner. Mulan returned to her hometown and was welcomed by her parents, brother and sister, and neighbors. Mulan went into her own room, changed into women's wear and did her hair before going out to meet the fellow soldiers, who were all astounded. They looked at each other and said: "Mulan has fought along with us for 12 years and we didn't know that she is a girl."

第九课

隋

隋朝（581年—618年）统一全国后，改变了选拔人才，任用官员的制度，废除了九品中正制，加强了中央集权。隋实行通过考试选拔人才的科举制，让出身低微而有才能的人通过读书也可以做官。

在经济制度方面，隋文帝沿用了北魏以来的均田制，使无田或少地的农民得到了土地。国家减轻了农民的税收和徭(yáo)役，生产力有了提高，社会经济出现了短暂的繁荣。短短20年间，隋的人口由3,000多万增至4,600多万；全国耕地面积增长一倍半，达到5,500多万顷；粮食丰收，国家建了许多粮仓，储存了大量粮食。

在手工业方面，纺织和造船业都很发达，造船的技术和规模在当时世界上是最先进的。为了加强全国各地间的联系，保证京城的粮食供

隋代五牙舰模型

给，隋炀帝时，用六年时间开凿了贯通南北的大运河。这条大运河南自余杭（今杭州），北到涿郡（今北京附近），全长约5,000里，成为中国南北交通的大动脉，是世界上最古老的一条人工大运河。

隋朝的疆域，东、南两面临海，北到今内蒙古，西至今新疆。隋统一全国后，还扩大了对外联系，与西域、南洋、日本往来频繁。中、日两国之间还互派使节，中国文化不断传播到日本。

隋朝的繁荣很短暂，由于统治者的腐化和暴政，隋政权迅速走向灭亡。炀帝时，大规模修建东都（洛阳），又修长城、修水渠、凿运河，并三次派兵出征高丽①，动用军队上百万，民工二三百万人，使农民离乡背井长期地去服兵役、运送军粮和武器，结果，土地荒芜，粮食短缺，农民没有活路，纷纷起来造反。当时主要的起义军有河北的窦建德、河南的瓦岗军。隋军节节败退。这时候，隋朝官员李渊等也起兵反隋。公元618年3月，隋炀帝被部下所杀，隋灭亡。

---

① 高丽——朝鲜历史上的王朝。

生词

zhōng yāng 中央	center		háng zhōu 杭州	Hangzhou (*capital city of Zhejiang Province*)
xuǎn bá 选拔	select			
dī wēi 低微	low-born		pín fán 频繁	frequent
duǎn zàn 短暂	temporary		bīng yì 兵役	military service
qǐng 顷	hectare		huāng wú 荒芜	go wild or waste
liáng cāng 粮仓	granary; barn		wǎ gāng jūn 瓦岗军	Wagang Army
chǔ cún 储存	store		lǐ yuān 李渊	Li Yuan (*name*)
guàn tōng 贯通	link up			

听写

短暂　粮仓　贯通　选拔　频繁　短缺　中央　储存

杭州　发达　*荒芜　兵役

比一比

缺 { 短缺 / 缺少 / 缺点

拔 { 选拔 / 提拔 / 拔牙

服 { 服兵役 / 服装 / 衣服

微 { 低微 / 微小 / 显微镜

暂 { 短暂 / 暂时 }　　繁 { 频繁 / 繁华 }　　仓 { 粮仓 / 仓库 }　　{ 贯（贯通）/ 惯（习惯）}

字词运用

巩固

隋统一全国以后，采取了一系列巩固政权的措施。

牢固

这座大桥的基础非常牢固。

缩短

巴拿马运河大大缩短了从美洲东海岸到亚洲间海运的距离。

短暂

莫扎特的一生虽然短暂，却留下了很多传世的音乐作品。

多音字

给 jǐ　　　　　给 gěi
供给 jǐ　　　　送给 gěi

回答问题

1. 隋朝开凿的大运河有多长？它北边到哪个城市，南边到哪个城市？

2. 什么是科举制？

词语解释

中央集权——中央，指国家最高领导部门；中央集权，指政治、经济、军事大权集中于中央。

人才——品德和才干都很好的人；也指有某种专业技能的人。

徭役——古时候，政府让人民承担的无偿(cháng)劳动。

离乡背井——离开故乡在外地生活。

短缺——不足，不够多。

造反——采取行动反抗统治。

节节败退——形容战争中一仗接一仗地不断失败、后退。

动脉——把心脏流出的血液送到全身各部分的血管。常用它比喻重要的交通干线。

大运河

　　大运河也叫京杭运河，是中国古代伟大的水利工程之一。大运河北起北京，南到杭州，中间经过天津、河北、山东、江苏、浙江等地。它沟通了海河、黄河、淮河、长江、钱塘江等大河。今天，大运河的长度为1,794千米。部分运河最早于公元前5世纪（春秋末期）开凿。公元605年到610年，隋炀帝为了加强对南北方的控制，方便南北方的物产交流，动用了几百万民工，花费了六年时间开凿了这条大运河。其中有些河段，是把以前挖好的运河加宽、加深，中间也利用一些天然河、湖相连结。隋代大运河全长2,000多千米，水面宽30～70米不等。运河对促进中国南北经济文化的交流和发展起了重要的作用。隋炀帝坐船从运河南下游玩，船队的船有上千艘，排起来在运河中有200多里长。

　　13世纪，元朝又开凿了

当代京杭大运河

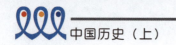

大都（今北京）到通州的一段运河，使运河从杭州一直通到北京。现在的运河只有部分河段可以通航。中国计划修复运河，主要想利用运河南水北调，解决北方缺水的问题。

qián táng jiāng		suí yáng dì	
钱塘江	Qiantangjiang River	隋炀帝	Emperor Yang of the Sui Dynasty

Lesson Nine

Sui Dynasty

After China was once again unified during the Sui Dynasty (581-618), the centralization of authority was greatly strengthened. As for official nomination, the original nine-level administrative system was abolished and was replaced by the imperial examination system, which made the official positions available to the low-born ordinary people by reading books.

In economical system, Sui Wendi adopted the land-equalization system since the Northern Wei Dynasty. The peasants without land or in possession of a small amount of land got allocated land; while at the same time the government also reduced their burden of taxes and corvee. Accordingly, the productivity had been greatly improved and there was temporary social and economic prosperity. In 20 years, the population increased from over 30 million to over 46 million, the area of arable land increased by 1.5 times and reached 55 million hectares. With plenteous harvest of grains, the government constructed a lot of granaries to store grains. In handicraft industry, both textile and boat building were highly developed; the techniques and scale of boat building ranked the first in the world at that time. In order to promote domestic contact and to guarantee sufficient food supplies to the capital city, during the reign of Sui Yangdi, it took people six years to construct the Grand Canal that linked the south and the north. The Grand Canal started from Yuhang (today's Hangzhou) in the south and ended in Zhuojun (near today's Beijing) in the north. It was 5,000 *li* long and became the most important transportation route in China. It is one of the greatest achievements of Chinese people.

The territory of Sui extended to the seas in both the east and the south, to today's Inner Mongolia in the north and to today's Xinjiang in the west. After Sui unified China, it also promoted foreign relations and had frequent communications with the Western Regions, the Southeast Asia and with Japan. China and Japan sent their respective envoys to the other country and Chinese culture kept spreading to Japan.

The prosperity of the Sui Dynasty lasted short due to corruption and tyranny of the rulers and the regime headed toward its end quickly. Under the reign of Yangdi (Emperor Yang), many large-scale construction projects were launched, including the construction of Eastern Capital (Luoyang), the Great Wall, the water channels and the Grand Canal. Meanwhile the government sent army to Koryo for three times. Several millions of soldiers and two to three millions of farmers were recruited. Accordingly, the peasants had long separated from the land, the land went wild and the food supplies were short. The peasants had no way out but to rebel against the government. The major forces at the time included the army led by Dou Jiande in Hebei and the Wagang army in Henan. The army of Sui government retreated in defeat step by step. At the same time, Li Yuan, an official of Sui, also rose up against Sui. In March 618AD, Emperor Yang was killed by his followers and this marked the end of the Sui Dynasty.

The Grand Canal

The Grand Canal, also known as Beijing-Hangzhou Canal, is one of the greatest ancient water conservancy projects in China. It starts from Beijing in the north and ends in Hangzhou in the south, passing Tianjin, Hebei, Shandong, Jiangsu, and Zhejiang, connecting the Haihe River, the Yellow River, the Huaihe River, the Yangtze River, and the Qiantangjiang River. Now its length is 1,794 kilometers. The Grand Canal was initially constructed in the 5th Century BC (at the end of the Spring and Autumn Period). From 605 to 610AD, in order to strengthen the control to both the south and the north and to facilitate material exchanges between the south and the north, Emperor Yang of the Sui Dynasty recruited several millions of laborers to construct the Grand Canal in six years. In some sections of the project, they merely widened and deepened the original canal; in some other sections, they made full use of the natural rivers and lakes to construct the canal. During the Sui Dynasty, the total length of the Grand Canal was more than 2,000 kilometers and its width varied from 30 meters to 70 meters. The canal was important to promote economic and cultural exchanges and development of the north and south China at the time. Emperor Yang traveled along the canal to the south in boat and his fleet was composed of more than one thousand boats of more than two hundred *li* long in the canal.

In the 13th Century during the Yuan Dynasty, the government once again constructed the part from Dadu (today's Beijing) to Tongzhou, thus the Grand Canal is navigable from Beijing to Hangzhou. Today, only part of the canal is navigable and China plans to repair it so as to divert water from the Yangtze River to North China and to solve the problem of water shortage in the north.

第十课

唐（上）

唐太宗李世民像

李渊出身于世代贵族家庭，与隋朝皇帝是亲戚，在儿子李世民的帮助下，于太原起兵反隋。公元618年，李渊在长安（今西安）称帝，国号唐。李世民是一个有雄才大略的人，他首先出兵西北地区，再往东，占领黄河南北。同时，派水陆大军进攻江南，统一全国。

唐朝（618年—907年）的国家制度是在隋朝的基础上发展完善的。唐还制定了一部成文法典《唐律疏议》，它成为后代法典的规范。唐还进一步发展了科举制，政府主要官员都是通过科举考试来选拔的。

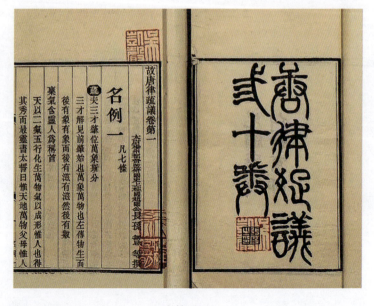

唐律疏议

武则天

唐仍然实行均田制，将荒废的土地分给农民，年满18岁的男子授田100亩（永业田20亩，口分(fēn)田80亩；口分田在人死后要交还国家），使农民重新回到田地里种田。唐又推行租庸(yōng)调制，按丁男征收赋税，也可以通过纳绢来代替服役。公元626年6月，李世民与兄长李建成争夺皇位成功，改年号①为贞观，他就是历史上有名的唐太宗。唐太宗善于听取别人意见，依法办事。他在位的时候，经济发展比较好，政治比较清明，史称"贞观之治"。唐太宗死后，继承皇位的唐高宗很懦弱，皇后武则天当政。公元690年，武后称帝，改国号为周，成为中国有史以来唯一的女皇帝。武则天打破了贵族当高官的老规矩，破格选用人才。武则天老年被迫退位，把权力交还给儿子，国号恢复为唐。

由于实行发展生产的政策，到唐玄宗时，社会经济高度繁荣。唐朝的水利灌溉工程多达254项，超过历代的总和。人口也增至5,288万。手工业不但种类多，而且水平高，以陶瓷而论，著名的"唐三彩"曾远销亚洲其他国家和非洲，是精美的艺术珍品。

---

① 为记载年代，从汉武帝开始，中国历代皇帝都立年号，立年号的第一年为元年，如贞观元年。

唐代商业繁荣，交通发达。陆路以长安为中心有通向全国四面八方的多条交通要道，道边共设驿站1,643所，正如后人所说，"处处有路通长安"。

唐朝打败东突厥①和西突厥，打通了往来西域的道路，并使天山南北广大地区全部纳入唐朝的版图。太宗还把文成公主嫁给吐蕃②首领松赞干布，唐蕃"同为一家"。唐还册封南诏（今云南）首领为云南王；并攻占了高丽，设置安东都护府。

胡人骑驼载乐俑（唐三彩）

高度发达的唐朝文化不但传到朝鲜、日本，而且通过中亚地区向西传播，比如造纸术就经阿拉伯人之手传到非洲和欧洲。同时外国文化也传到中国，促进了中外交流。唐初，僧人玄奘历尽艰苦到印度学习佛法，回国后把佛经译成汉语。神话小说《西游记》就是根据玄奘"取经"的故事创作的。

唐的强盛和开放，使这个朝代在全世界产生了很大的影响，一些西方国家华人聚居的地方至今还被称为"唐人街"。

---

① 突厥——中国古代少数民族，游牧在阿尔泰山一带。西魏时建立政权，后被唐灭。
② 吐蕃——中国古代少数民族，居住在今青藏高原。唐时曾建立政权。

生词

(谋)略 móu lüè	stratgem	
法典 fǎ diǎn	statute book	
授 shòu	confer; give	
丁男 dīng nán	male adult	
赋税 fù shuì	tax	
绢 juàn	thin silk	
贞观 zhēn guān	the reign title of Emperor Taizong of the Tang Dynasty	
懦弱 nuò ruò	coward; weak	
破格 pò gé	break the convention	
政策 zhèng cè	policy	
唐玄宗 táng xuán zōng	Emperor Xuanzong of the Tang Dynasty	
驿站 yì zhàn	post	
聚居 jù jū	live in a compact community	

听写

谋略　法典　政策　（教）授　聚居　绢　破格　玄　强盛　*懦弱

比一比

典 { 法典　经典　典礼

破 { 破格　破产　突破

历 { 历代　历史　来历

居 { 居民 / 邻居   精 { 精美 / 精神   政 { 政策 / 政府   { 授（教授） / 受（难受）

字词运用

代替

张老师病了，今天王老师代替她上课。

善于

他不善于说话，但是文章写得很好。

艰苦

远古的时候，人类经常吃不饱，穿不暖，生活很艰苦。

聚居

美国旧金山是亚裔聚居的城市。

居民

中国的上海有一千七百多万居民,是世界上最大的城市之一。

回答问题

1. 唐朝是在哪一年建立的?
2. 唐太宗的名字叫什么?
3. 唐太宗把文成公主嫁给了谁?
4. 唐朝的时候中国有多少人口?
5. 中国历史上唯一的女皇帝是谁?
6. 唐朝僧人玄奘到印度去做什么?

词语解释

雄才大略——杰出的才智和谋略。

贞观之治——唐太宗时,政治开明,经济发展,社会安定,国力强盛。史学家把这一时期称为"贞观之治"。

阅读

（一）玄奘

　　玄奘于公元602年出生在河南。他是一位佛学大师，也是佛经翻译家和旅行家。玄奘原名陈祎，13岁就在洛阳出家，专心研究佛学。后来他云游四方，遍访名师，24岁到了长安。在佛学研究的过程中，他发现许多经典的翻译有错误。他听说天竺（古印度）有很多佛经，于是决心西游。公元627年，他独自离开长安西行取经，经受了各种艰难和危险，最终到达印度。他刻苦学习佛教，受到了印度各界的尊敬。玄奘西行前后17年，回到长安时，受到数十万人欢迎。玄奘用20匹马运回佛经657部。在玄奘的主持下，唐朝政府在长安开设译场。花了19年的时间，玄奘译出梵文经典75部，共1,335卷。他还将一些汉语经典，如老子的《道德经》译成了梵文。

　　玄奘还是伟大的旅行家，他不怕艰难，行走了25,000多千米，经过了138个国家。回国以后，他把一路的上所见所闻

玄奘取经图

及在印度的生活写在《大唐西域记》一书中。《大唐西域记》真实地记录了7世纪印度、尼泊尔等地的地理环境、山川河流、气候、物产、城市、交通道路、种族、人口、风土民情、宗教信仰、衣食住行、政治、文化等等。这些记录成为研究这些地方和国家古代历史的宝贵资料。这本书写得十分生动，成为世界名著。玄奘去印度取经，促使唐朝与中亚、西亚、印度的交往迅速发展。

（二）文成公主和松赞干布

松赞干布（617年—650年）是吐蕃的一个国王。他一直仰慕唐朝的灿烂文化。为了加强与唐朝的联系，学习汉族地区的先进文化，松赞干布派使臣到唐朝求婚。唐太宗同意将文成公主嫁给松赞干布。公元641年，松赞干布在黄河的源头扎陵湖边，迎取了美丽的文成公主。文成公主进入西藏时，将中原地区的农具制造技术和纺织、建筑、造纸、酿酒、制陶、冶金等生产技术，都带到吐蕃，还带去了汉族地区种植的粮食、蔬菜的种子，并且把种植方法也教给了吐蕃人。这极大地促进了

松赞干布与文成公主塑像

吐蕃各种技术和文化的发展。松赞干布为了学习更多的中原文化，还派吐蕃青年到长安学习。

生词

chén yī 陈祎	Chen Yi (*name*)	xìn yǎng 信仰	belief
tiān zhú 天竺	Tianzhu (*ancient India*)	càn làn 灿烂	brilliant; splenid
fàn wén 梵文	Sanskrit	tǔ bō 吐蕃	Tubo (*ancient Tibet*)
zōng jiào 宗教	religion	niàng jiǔ 酿酒	brew

译文 English Translation

Lesson Ten

Tang (I)

Li Yuan was born in an aristocratic family that lasted for generations and was a relative to the emperors of the Sui Dynasty. With the help of his son Li Shimin, he rose up in Taiyuan against Sui and ascended to throne in 618AD in Chang'an (today's Xi'an). The title of the reigning dynasty was Tang. Li Shimin was an ambitious man with great talent and bold vision. He firstly led army to take over the northwestern area and then headed toward the east to capture the areas to the south and the north of the Yellow River. While at the same time, he also sent armies from both land and water to attack the area to the south of the Yangtze River and finally unified the entire country.

The state systems of the Tang Dynasty (618-907) were developed on the basis of those in the Sui Dynasty. Its written code of *The Law of Tang* set the standard for the later generations in the field. In addition, it further developed the imperial examination system and most of the governmental officials were chosen through examinations. Tang adopted the land-equalization system and distributed the waste

land without owner to the peasants. Men of 18 years old would be granted 100 *mu* lands (20 *mu* for permanent ownership and 80 *mu* for provisions that would be returned to the government after the owner died) and this effectively guaranteed that peasants were back to the land. Then the government adopted the system of levying taxes and corvee on the basis of equalizing land. The taxes were levied according to the number of male adult in a family and the corvee labor could be replaced by think silk. In June 626AD, Li Shimin organized a coup d'etat and successfully ascended to the throne by changing the title of the emperor's reign into Zhenguan. He was the famous Tang Taizong in the history of China. Taizong was good at listening to others and handling affairs according to laws. Under his reign, the economy flourished and the politics was clean and just. This period of time was known as the Reign of Zhenguan in history. After Taizong died, his son Gaozong was weak and the country was actually ruled by Wu Zetian, the empress. In 690AD, Empress Wu ascended to the throne and changed the title of the reigning dynasty into Zhou, becoming the only empress in power in the history of China. Wu Zetian broke the convention that only noblemen could be senior officials and promoted low-born officials, which had progressive significance. In her later days, she was force to give up the throne and handed the power back to her son Tang Zhongzong and the name of Tang thus resumed.

Thanks to the policies of promoting production, till the reign of Tang Xuanzong, the society and economy highly flourished. There were as many as 254 water conservancy and irrigation projects in the Tang Dynasty, which was more than the total number of those in all past dynasties. The population increased to 52.88 million. The handicraft industry fell into various categories and all of them were developed in a high level. Taking pottery and porcelain as an example, the famous Tri-colored Pottery of Tang was popular in the markets of Asia, Africa and other countries, and was the most refined artistic treasure. During the Tang Dynasty, the business boomed, the transportation was developed with many main lines on land centering on the capital city of Chang'an and leading to the entire country with a total of 1,643 post-houses. Later generations described it: "There are roads leading to Chang'an everywhere."

Tang defeated the Eastern and Western Turks so as to clear the road leading to the Western Regions and included the vast areas to the south and north of the Tianshan Mountain into the territory of Tang. Taizong also married Princess Wencheng to Songtsan Gambo, the chieftain of Tubo, so as to unite Tang and Tubo as one big family. Tang government also conferred the title of Yunnan King on the chieftain of Nanzhao (today's Yunnan), attacked and defeated Koryo, and established Andong Protectorate (du-hu-fu) there.

The highly developed Tang culture was widely spread in Korea, Japan and to the west through Middle Asia. For example, the technique of making paper was introduced to Africa and Europe through Arabians. While at the same time, foreign cultures were also communicated to China and the exchanges between China and foreign countries were greatly promoted. At the beginning of the Tang Dynasty, monk Xuan Zang traveled a long way to India to learn Buddhist doctrine, and translated Buddhist Scriptures into Chinese after he returned. The mythological novel *Journey to the West* (also known as *the Monkey King*) was based on the stories of Xuan Zang going on a pilgrimage for Buddhist sutra.

The prosperity and openness of Tang make it one of the most influential dynasties in the world and the places where overseas Chinese gather in western countries are still known as Tang People Street (Chinatown).

Xuan Zang

Xuan Zang was born in Henan in 602AD. He was a master in Buddhism, a translator of Buddhist scriptures and a traveler as well. Xuan Zang was originally Chen Yi and became a monk at 13 to devote in the study of Buddhism. He then roamed around seeking for prestigious masters and went to Chang'an at 24. During his study, he found a lot of mistakes in the translation of Buddhist scriptures. He heard that there were a lot of Buddhist scriptures kept in Tianzhu (ancient India) and accordingly made up his mind to go on a pilgrimage to the west. In 627AD, he left Chang'an heading toward the west for Buddhist scriptures. Having experienced many hardships, he finally arrived in India and worked hard at learning Buddhism. He was widely respected among Indians at the time. Seventeen years later, Xuan Zang returned to Chang'an and was welcome by hundreds of thousands of people there. Xuan Zang carried 675 Buddhist scriptures with 20 horses and was then in charge of the governmental project of scripture translation in Chang'an. During next 19 years, Xuan Zang translated 75 volumes and 1,335 books of sutra from Sanskrit into Chinese. At the same time, he also translated some Chinese classics into Sanskrit including *Tao Teh Ching* by Laozi.

Xuan Zang was a great traveler. He traveled 25,000 kilometers, passed 138 countries and recorded all his travel experience as well as his life in India in Journey to India in *the Great Tang Dynasty*. In his book, Xuan Zang recorded the geography, mountains and rivers, climate, products, cities, transportation and roads, races and people, natural conditions and social customs, religions and beliefs, clothing, food, houses and transportation vehicles, politics and cultures of India and Nepal in the 7th Century. These now become the precious materials for us to study the ancient history of these regions and countries. The language of the book is vivid and it is now one of the world literary classics. Xuan Zang went on a pilgrimage for Buddhist scriptures in India and promoted the exchanges between Tang and the Middle Asia, the Western Asia, and India.

Princess Wencheng and Songtsan Gambo

Songtsan Gambo (617-650) was a king of Tubo and had high respect for brilliant cultures of the Tang Dynasty. In order to strengthen the relations with Tang and to learn from the advanced culture of Han nationality, Songtsan Gambo sent envoys to Chang'an to make an offer of marriage. Tang Taizong then agreed to marry Princess Wencheng to Songtsan Gambo. In 641AD, Songtsan Gambo married beautiful Princess Wencheng besides the Gyaring Lake, the source of the Yellow River. Princess Wencheng brought the techniques of producing agricultural tools, weaving, constructing, paper making, brewing, potting and metallurgy to Tubo, and taught local people the methods of growing grains and vegetables, which greatly improved the techniques and cultures of Tubo. In order to learn more about the culture the central plains, Songtsan Gambo also sent young men to Chang'an to study there.

生字表(简)

1. 谋(móu) 猿(yuán) 烬(jìn) 址(zhǐ)
2. 尧(yáo) 启(qǐ) 隶(lì) 监(jiān) 狱(yù) 铸(zhù) 率(shuài) 滨(bīn) 侯(hóu) 幽(yōu)
3. 霸(bà) 邀(yāo) 孝(xiào) 爵(jué) 奖(jiǎng) 励(lì) 耕(gēng) 冶(yě)
4. 郡(jùn) 廷(tíng) 亭(tíng) 申(shēn) 纳(nà) 税(shuì) 币(bì) 轨(guǐ) 巩(gǒng) 巡(xún) 逮(dǎi) 刑(xíng) 项(xiàng)
5. 租(zū) 恢(huī) 削(xuē) 铢(zhū) 廊(láng) 琳(lín) 琅(láng) 喀(kā) 裔(yì)
6. 坝(bà) 播(bō) 仲(zhòng) 佗(tuó) 疾(jí) 标(biāo) 阀(fá)
7. 袁(yuán) 屯(tún) 昌(chāng) 局(jú) 措(cuò) 贷(dài) 款(kuǎn) 购(gòu) 执(zhí)
8. 汝(rǔ) 奢(shē) 侈(chǐ) 蜡(là) 陷(xiàn) 裕(yù) 卑(bēi) 驳(bó) 绘(huì)
9. 央(yāng) 顷(qǐng) 储(chǔ) 贯(guàn) 杭(háng) 频(pín) 役(yì) 羌(wú) 岗(gāng) 渊(yuān)
10. 略(lüè) 授(shòu) 赋(fù) 绢(juàn) 贞(zhēn) 懦(nuò) 玄(xuán) 驿(yì) 聚(jù)

共计88个生字

生字表（繁）

1. 謀(móu) 猿(yuán) 燼(jìn) 址(zhǐ)
2. 堯(yáo) 啟(qǐ) 隸(lì) 監(jiān) 獄(yù) 鑄(zhù) 率(shuài) 濱(bīn) 侯(hóu) 幽(yōu)
3. 霸(bà) 邀(yāo) 孝(xiào) 爵(jué) 獎(jiǎng) 勵(lì) 耕(gēng) 冶(yě)
4. 郡(jùn) 廷(tíng) 亭(tíng) 申(shēn) 納(nà) 稅(shuì) 幣(bì) 軌(guǐ) 鞏(gǒng) 巡(xún) 逮(dǎi) 刑(xíng) 項(xiàng)
5. 租(zū) 恢(huī) 削(xuē) 銖(zhū) 廊(láng) 琳(lín) 琅(láng) 喀(kā) 裔(yì)
6. 壩(bà) 播(bō) 仲(zhòng) 佗(tuó) 疾(jí) 標(biāo) 閥(fá)
7. 袁(yuán) 屯(tún) 昌(chāng) 局(jú) 措(cuò) 貸(dài) 款(kuǎn) 購(gòu) 執(zhí)
8. 汝(rǔ) 奢(shē) 侈(chǐ) 蠟(là) 陷(xiàn) 裕(yù) 卑(bēi) 駁(bó) 繪(huì)
9. 央(yāng) 頃(qǐng) 儲(chǔ) 貫(guàn) 杭(háng) 頻(pín) 役(yì) 蕪(wú) 崗(gāng) 淵(yuān)
10. 略(lüè) 授(shòu) 賦(fù) 絹(juàn) 貞(zhēn) 懦(nuò) 玄(xuán) 驛(yì) 聚(jù)

共計88個生字

生词表（简）

1. 独立 考古 元谋 猿人 陆续 灰烬 完整 装饰
   观念 氏族 繁荣 部落 联盟 联合 遗址

2. 尧 启 奴隶 监狱 铸造 水平 残暴 率领 海滨
   诸侯 周幽王

3. 支持 称霸 改革 邀请 程度 孝 废除 官爵
   奖励 耕（地） 普遍 冶（炼） 规模 流通 动荡
   争论 解放

4. 郡县 朝廷 亭 申报 纳税 法律 货币 轨（道）
   巩固 巡游 逮捕 征服 刑罚 谋害 项

5. 释放 田租 恢复 削弱 五铢钱 专卖 打击
   国际贸易 走廊 居民 琳琅满目 巴尔喀什 版图
   破产 腐败 占领 后裔

6. 堤坝 传播 动态 张仲景 华佗 传染病 免费
   治疗 疾病 外科 摆脱 管辖 目的地 危机 标志
   坚持 镇压 军阀 政权

7. 袁绍 收编 屯田 许昌 建议 局面 改进 措施
   贷款 购买 执政 战乱 装载 投降 分裂

8. 汝南王 奢侈 伙食费 彼此 蜡 迁移 瓦解 陷入
   刘裕 鲜卑 融合 批驳 绘画 圆周率

9. 中央 选拔 低微 短暂 顷 粮仓 储存 贯通
   杭州 频繁 兵役 荒芜 瓦岗军 李渊

10. (谋)略 法典 授 丁男 赋税 绢 贞观 懦弱
    破格 政策 唐玄宗 驿站 聚居

共计 151 个生词

生詞表（繁）

1. 獨立 考古 元謀 猿人 陸續 灰燼 完整 裝飾
   觀念 氏族 繁榮 部落 聯盟 聯合 遺址

2. 堯 啟 奴隸 監獄 鑄造 水平 殘暴 率領 海濱
   諸侯 周幽王

3. 支持 稱霸 改革 邀請 程度 孝 廢除 官爵
   獎勵 耕（地） 普遍 冶（煉） 規模 流通 動蕩
   爭論 解放

4. 郡縣 朝廷 亭 申報 納稅 法律 貨幣 軌（道）
   鞏固 巡遊 逮捕 征服 刑罰 謀害 項

5. 釋放 田租 恢復 削弱 五銖錢 專賣 打擊
   國際貿易 走廊 居民 琳琅滿目 巴爾喀什 版圖
   破產 腐敗 佔領 後裔

6. 堤壩 傳播 動態 張仲景 華佗 傳染病 免費
   治療 疾病 外科 擺脫 管轄 目的地 危機 標誌
   堅持 鎮壓 軍閥 政權

中国历史（上）

7. 袁紹 收編 屯田 許昌 建議 局面 改進 措施
   貸款 購買 執政 戰亂 裝載 投降 分裂

8. 汝南王 奢侈 伙食費 彼此 蠟 遷移 瓦解 陷入
   劉裕 鮮卑 融合 批駁 繪畫 圓周率

9. 中央 選拔 低微 短暫 頃 糧倉 儲存 貫通
   杭州 頻繁 兵役 荒蕪 瓦崗軍 李淵

10. (謀)略 法典 授 丁男 賦稅 絹 貞觀 懦弱
    破格 政策 唐玄宗 驛站 聚居

共計 151 個生詞

中国历史朝代年表

夏　约公元前 21 世纪——约公元前 17 世纪

商　约公元前 17 世纪——约公元前 11 世纪

周　西周　约公元前 11 世纪——公元前 771 年

　　东周　公元前 770 年——公元前 256 年

　　　春秋时代　公元前 770 年——公元前 476 年

　　　战国时代　公元前 475 年——公元前 221 年

秦　公元前 221 年——公元前 206 年

汉　西汉　公元前 206 年——公元 25 年

　　东汉　公元 25 年——公元 220 年

三国（魏蜀吴）公元 220 年——公元 280 年

西晋　公元 265 年——公元 317 年

东晋 十六国　公元 317 年——公元 420 年

南北朝　公元 420 年——公元 589 年

隋 公元581年——公元618年

唐 公元618年——公元907年

五代十国 公元907年——公元960年

宋 北宋 公元960年——公元1127年

　　南宋 公元1127年——公元1279年

辽 公元916年——公元1125年

西夏 公元1038年——公元1227年

金 公元1115年——公元1234年

元 公元1271年——公元1368年

明 公元1368年——公元1644年

清 公元1644年——公元1911年

第一课

一 写生词

元	谋											

猿	人											

灰	烬											

遗	址											

二 组词

装_____　　猿_____　　饰_____　　普_____

吞_____　　庭_____　　联_____　　民_____

古_____　　址_____　　独_____　　整_____

氏族_____　　始_____　　观_____　　盟_____

三 选字组词

地（止　址）　　（猿　元）猴　　（合　和）并

人（明　民）　　（装　庄）饰　　（晋　普）通

(服 裤)装　　　　村(装 庄)　　　　富(强 虽)

(包 饱)装　　　　陆(读 续)　　　　联(和 合)

联(细 系)　　　　独(立 力)　　　　完(正 整)

四 写出反义词

饿——　　　　　　　　得——

减——　　　　　　　　高——

五 根据课文选择正确答案

1. 中国三面被高原、山脉环绕，一面是海洋，环境 _____。

　　A 四通八达　　　　　　B 相对独立

2. 考古证明，在170万年以前，中国大地上 _____。

　　A 还没有原始人类　　　B 已经有了原始人类

3. 北京周口店附近发现的50万年前的古人类头骨化石，我们把这些原始人称为_____。

　　A "山顶洞人"　　　　　B "北京人"

4. 公元前6,000年左右,黄河中下游地区普遍存在着农业文化。这个时期是_____。

   A 母系氏族社会　　　　　　B 父系氏族社会

5. 炎帝部落和黄帝部落存在于_____。

   A 约4,000多年前　　　　　B 约6,000多年前

6. 中华民族的祖先是_____。

   A 蚩(chī)尤　　B 皇帝　　C 黄帝　　D 上帝

六　造句

1. 家庭_____

2. 完整_____

3. 普遍_____

七　根据阅读材料选择填空

1. 黄帝姓_____,名轩辕。（姬　黄）

2. 黄帝生活在大约_____年前。(4,600　6,400)

3. 黄帝的部落居住在中国_____流域的黄土高原上。

（黄河　长江）

4. 居住在山东的九黎部落首领叫_____。

（蚩尤　炎帝）

5. 先是炎帝与蚩尤两个部落发生了战争,结果蚩尤_____。 (胜了　败了)

6. 蚩尤有81个兄弟,个个都十分_____。 (软弱　勇猛)

7. 炎黄部落联盟和九黎部落打仗,蚩尤战败_____。 (被杀　被抓)

8. 炎帝部落和黄帝部落又打了一仗,炎帝_____,于是两个部落合并。 (失败　胜了)

9. 传说黄帝还是一个发明家。他教人们_____。 (盖房子　用火做饭)

10. 黄帝的妻子嫘(léi)祖发明了_____。 (养猪　养蚕)

11. 传说,黄帝的史官仓颉(jié)创造了_____。 (文字　文学)

12. 中国人也自称_____。 (炎黄子孙　炎帝子孙)

八　缩写《黄帝的故事》(200字左右)

_____

_____

_____

九 回答问题(选做题)

你知道尧、舜、禹这三个人吗？如果知道,请简单讲一讲关于他们的事情。

答：

十 熟读课文

第三课

一 写生词

称霸											
邀请											
孝											
官爵											
奖励											
耕地											
冶炼											

二 组词

霸_____   耕_____   袭_____   程_____

奖_____   荡_____   改_____   规_____

推_____   废_____   邀_____   冶_____

支_____   解_____   励_____   普_____

三 选字组词

（任　人）用　　　（废　发）除　　　（平　苹）衡

（任　人）何　　　头（废　发）　　　（平　苹）果

奖（励　力）　　　普（骗　遍）　　　（冶　治）炼

努（励　力）　　　（骗　遍）人　　　（冶　治）病

四 选择填空

1. 美国早就_____了黑奴制。（废除　废物）

2. 虽然拆下来的包装纸是_____，但是可以利用。

（废除　废物）

3. 燕山石油化工厂_____很大，有几万工人。

（规模　规矩）

4. 考试要守_____，不要偷看别人的答案。

（规模　规矩）

5. 大家有不同意见，可以_____。（争论　争吵）

6. 请不要大声_____，说话要注意礼貌。

（争论　争吵）

7. 我们大家_____你做班长。（支持　保持）

8. 青藏高原上氧气少，请注意_____体力。
（yǎng）

（支持　保持）

五 根据课文选择正确答案

1. 东周这段历史一般分为_____两个时期。

   A 西周和东周　　　B 东汉和西汉　　　C 春秋和战国

2. 春秋时期的特点是_____。

   A 和平　　　B 诸侯争霸　　　C 小国称霸

3. 春秋初年,诸侯国有_____。

   A 7个　　　B 20多个　　　C 100多个

4. 春秋时期首先称霸的是_____。

   A 齐桓(huán)公　　B 秦孝公　　C 管仲(zhòng)　　D 周天子

5. "战国七雄"是:_____。

   A 齐、楚、燕、韩、赵、魏、秦　　　B 齐、楚、燕、韩、宋、魏、秦

6. 下面哪一条不是商鞅(yāng)变法的内容?_____

   A 废除官爵世袭制度　　　B 奖励作战有功的人

   C 分封诸侯

   D 实行土地私有,土地可以自由买卖

   E 统一度量衡

7. 秦国先后灭掉六国,_____。

   A 打败了蒙古　　　　　B 统一了中国

六 造句

    1. 奖励_____

    2. 邀请_____

    3. 支持_____

七 根据阅读材料判断对错

    1. 商鞅是战国时期的政治家,秦国人。　　___对　___错

    2. 商鞅认为追求名利是人的本性,提出"利出于地,名出于战"。　　___对　___错

    3. 商鞅在变法前,花重金让人搬木头。　　___对　___错

    4. 新法统一了度量衡,便利了商业往来。　　___对　___错

    5. 新法一公布,秦国的旧贵族都欢迎。　　___对　___错

    6. 秦孝公死前,商鞅被贵族杀害。　　___对　___错

八 熟读课文

第五课

一 写生词

田	租										
恢	复										
削	弱										
五	铢	钱									
走	廊										
后	裔										
琳	琅	满	目								
巴	尔	喀	什								

二 组词

释_____ 租_____ 恢_____ 削_____

专_____ 裔_____ 版_____ 廊_____

击_____ 腐_____ 描_____ 勤_____

职_____ 占_____ 居_____ 琳琅_____

三 选字组词

（组 租）织　　（恢 灰）烬　　（削 消）弱

田（组 租）　　（恢 灰）复　　（削 消）灭

房（顶 盯）　　（传 专）门　　走（郎 廊）

华（衣 裔）　　（专 传）统　　女（郎 廊）

四 写出反义词

增强——　　　　加重——

五 选择填空

1.这次试验的失败对科学家们是一次很大的_____。

（袭击　打击）

2. 他从监狱里_____出来，满怀希望地开始了新生活。

(解释　释放)

3. 他们不是本地的_____，是来这里的旅游者。

(居住　居民)

4. 许多国家都有政治_____的问题。

(腐败　腐烂　豆腐)

5. _____的食物不能吃。(腐败　腐烂　豆腐)

6. 多吃_____有助健康。(腐败　腐烂　豆腐)

六　根据课文选择正确答案

1. _____建立西汉王朝。

　　A 汉武帝　　　B 刘邦　　　C 张骞(qiān)　　　D 秦始皇

2. 刘邦接受秦灭亡的教训，_____。

　　A 让百姓休养生息　　　B 让百姓出征打仗

3. 汉武帝时，在思想上_____。

　　A 百家争鸣　　　B 罢黜(chù)百家

4. 西汉时，_____农具使用很普遍。

　　A 木头　　　B 铁制　　　C 青铜

5. 西汉时，手工_____已经达到很高水平。

　　A 冶铁和纺织业　　B 农业　　　C 造船业

6. 西汉时,张骞出使西域,开通了一条国际贸易路线,它就是历史上有名的_____。

   A"丝绸之路"   B"茶叶之路"   C"香料之路"

七 造句

恢复_____

八 词语解释

琳琅满目——

九 根据阅读材料判断对错

1. 汉武帝派张骞出使西域。　　　　　　　　　___对　___错

2. 那时的西域,指玉门关以西,直至中亚、
   南亚和西亚一带。　　　　　　　　　　　___对　___错

3. 张骞第一次去西域时被匈奴抓住。　　　　___对　___错

4. 张骞在匈奴住了十多年,他掌握了
   匈奴的情况。　　　　　　　　　　　　　___对　___错

5. 张骞第二次出使西域,使汉朝同西域
   各国建立了联系。　　　　　　　　　　　___对　___错

十 请写一写张骞出使西域在历史上的意义

十一 熟读课文

第七课

一 写生词

袁	绍										
屯	田										
许	昌										
局	面										
措	施										
贷	款										
购	买										
执	政										

二 组词

款_____ 议_____ 措_____ 执_____

局_____ 投_____ 稳_____ 贷_____

败_____ 操_____ 购_____ 改_____

三 选字组词

许（昌　冒）　　（局　居）面　　（购　钩）子

（昌　冒）烟　　（局　居）民　　（购　钩）买

排（列　裂）　　（措　错）施　　装（栽　载）

分（列　裂）　　（措　错）误　　（栽　载）花

四 挑选并写出反义词

危险　降　发放　问　向　出现

答——　　　　收回——　　　　背——

安全——　　　消失——　　　　升——

五 根据课文选择正确答案

1. 曹操南下，想吞并江南，_____。

　　A 统一全中国　　　B 统一全世界

2. 刘备接受军师诸葛亮的建议，_____。

　　A 拼死抗曹　　B 与曹操结盟　　C 与孙权结盟，共同抗曹

3. 曹军20万人与孙刘联军5万余人在_____开战。

　　A 黄河边　　　B 湖南　　　C 赤壁　　　D 河南

4. 孙刘联军用_____打败了曹军。

   A 攻城　　　　　B 火攻　　　　　C 水攻

5. 赤壁之战后,刘备建立了_____。

   A 蜀国　　　　　B 吴国　　　　　C 魏国

6. 三国是指_____。

   A 魏、蜀、秦　　B 魏、蜀、汉　　C 魏、蜀、吴

7. 曹操提出"唯才是举",意思是_____。

   A 重用有才干的人　　　　B 重用有地位、有钱的人

   C 重用自己家的人

8. 吴国手工业有所发展,当时制造的大海船能装载_____
   _____。

   A 大约700人　　B 大约7,000人　　C 大约300人

六　选词填空

　　　　建设　　建议　　生存　　存在　　贷款　　措施

1. 我们应该注意保护人类的_____环境。

2. 爸爸向银行_____给家里买房子。

3. 医生_____妈妈要注意饮食和加强锻炼。

4. 海南岛已_____成为一个现代化的旅游区。

5. 医院已经制定了防止流感的_____。

6. 目前的教学方法不够好，还_____一些问题。

七 造句

1. 建议_____

2. 购买_____

八 根据阅读材料判断对错

1. 曹操统一中国后，发展生产，增强了兵力。 ___对 ___错

2. 曹操率领20万大军南下，想消灭刘备和孙权，统一全国。 ___对 ___错

3. 当时刘备和孙权只有5万兵马。 ___对 ___错

4. 曹操的兵多数是北方人，他们不会游泳，并且晕船。 ___对 ___错

5. 曹操采用了"连环船"的办法，人在上面走就像在平地上走一样。 ___对 ___错

6. 孙刘联军无法战胜"连环船"。 ___对 ___错

7. 黄盖带领的小船上装满了干草和粮食，

到了离曹营不远的地方就放火烧船。 ___对 ___错

8. 赤壁之战曹军大败。 ___对 ___错

九 熟读课文

第九课

一 写生词

中	央									
顷										
储	存									
贯	通									
杭	州									
频	繁									
兵	役									
荒	芜									
瓦	岗	军								
李	渊									

二 组词

杭_____　　役_____　　暂_____　　仓_____

央_____　　贯_____　　频_____　　荒_____

缺_____　　戚_____　　储_____　　拔_____

三 选字组词

粮（舱　仓）　　（暂　站）时　　（频　瓶）繁

船（舱　仓）　　短（暂　站）　　（频　瓶）子

荒（芜　无）　　（杭　抗）州　　兵（役　没）

（芜　无）论　　抵（杭　抗）　　（役　没）有

四 挑选并写出反义词

缩小　主人　落　送　腐烂

客人——　　　　涨——　　　　放大——

新鲜——　　　　迎——

五 根据课文选择正确答案

1. 隋朝统一全国后，任用官员的制度实行了_____。

　　A 九品中正制　　　B 科举制　　　C 禅让

2. 科举制使_____通过读书也可以做官。

   A 出身低微的人　　　B 有钱的人　　　C 王公贵族

3. 隋朝社会经济出现了_____繁荣。

   A 长期的　　　　　　B 短暂的

4. 隋文帝时,粮食丰收,国家建了许多粮仓,_____了大量粮食。

   A 存钱　　　　　　　B 储存　　　　　C 存车

5. 隋朝时,纺织和造船业都很发达,造船技术和规模在当时世界上是_____。

   A 中等的　　　　　　B 最落后的　　　C 最先进的

6. 为了加强全国各地间的联系,保证京城的粮食供给,隋炀(yáng)帝的时候,用了_____时间开凿了大运河。

   A 十年　　　　　　　B 三年　　　　　C 六年

7. 大运河,南自余杭(今杭州),北到涿郡(今北京附近),全长_____。

   A 5,000多里　　　　B 5,000多千米　 C 500多千米

8. 隋统一全国后,扩大了对外联系,与西域、南洋、日本往来频繁,中、日两国之间还互派_____,中国文化不断传播到日本。

   A 教师　　　　B 商人　　　C 使节　　　D 和尚

六 选词填空

　　　　频繁　繁殖　短缺　头等舱　贯通

1. 大运河_____中国南北。

2. 飞机有经济舱、商务舱和_____。

3. 去年夏天我们这里电力_____，许多家庭不能开空调。

4. 老鼠_____得很快。

5. 北京的首都机场是世界上最大的机场之一，每天飞机的起飞和降落都十分_____。

七 词语解释

1. 科举制 ——
2. 贯通 ——
3. 频繁 ——

八 根据阅读材料判断对错

1. 大运河也叫京杭运河，是中国古代伟大的水利工程之一。　　　　___对　___错

2. 大运河北起北京，南到上海。　　　　___对　___错

3. 隋代大运河全长2,000多千米,水面宽
   30～70米不等。　　　　　　　　　　___对　___错

4. 大运河促进了中国南北经济文化的
   交流和发展。　　　　　　　　　　　___对　___错

5. 隋炀帝坐船从运河南下游玩,船队排
   起来在运河中有20多里长。　　　　___对　___错

6. 13世纪元朝又修复大运河,使运河从
   北京直通到苏州。　　　　　　　　　___对　___错

7. 现在的运河还可以全线通航。　　　　___对　___错

九　熟读课文

第一课听写

第三课听写

第五课听写

第七课听写

第九课听写

中国历史（上）

第二课

一 写生词

尧											
启											
奴	隶										
监	狱										
铸	造										
率	领										
海	滨										
诸	侯										
周	幽	王									

二 组词

奴_____   率_____   监_____   庞_____

铸_____   诸_____   暴_____   滨_____

三 选字组词

（坚　监）狱　　　（奴　努）力　　　（率　摔）领

（坚　监）强　　　（奴　努）隶　　　（率　摔）碎

四 选词填空

疆土　积累　海滨　暴风雨　信封

1. 请把信写好后装进_____，贴上邮票，再寄出去。

2. 中国海南岛的_____非常美丽，那里四季常绿，海水蔚(wèi)蓝。

3. _____过后，许多房屋被损坏了。

4. 中国的_____很辽阔。

5. 掌握知识要靠慢慢地学习和_____。

五 根据课文选择正确答案

1. 中国历史上第一个王朝是_____。

　　A 商　　　B 周　　　C 夏　　　D 秦　　　E 汉

2. 谁建立了夏？答案是_____。

　　A 尧　　　B 炎帝　　　C 黄帝　　　D 禹

3. 夏是中国历史上第一个_____国家。

    A 分封诸侯的　　　　B 奴隶制　　　　C 封建制

4. 夏的疆土主要在今_____。

    A 河南、山西一带　　B 中国南方　　　C 山东

5. 青铜器司母戊(wù)鼎重875公斤,是_____朝制造的。

    A 周　　　B 唐　　　C 商　　　D 夏

6. 商代出现了刻在龟甲、兽骨上的文字,后人称它为_____。

    A 甲骨文　　　　B 金文

六 造句

　　属于_____

七 词语解释

　　1. 庞大——

　　2. 积累——

八 根据阅读材料判断对错

1. 甲骨文是3,000多年前中国商代使用的文字。　　___对　___错

2. 商朝灭亡后,祖庙和档案馆都倒塌了,经过漫长的岁月,废墟又被覆上厚厚的黄土,甲骨文几乎没有人知道了。　　___对　___错

3. 1899年,一位学者从西药中发现了甲骨文。　　___对　___错

4. 河南安阳郊外的小屯,3,000多年前曾经是夏朝的国都。　　___对　___错

5. 甲骨文共有约4,500多单字,已形成一个较完整的文字体系。　　___对　___错

6. 现在科学家们已经完全认出甲骨文了。___对　___错

九 请写一写甲骨文是怎样被发现的(150字左右)

_____
_____
_____

十　熟读课文

第四课

一 写生词

郡	县										
朝	廷										
亭											
申	报										
纳	税										
货	币										
轨	道										
巩	固										
巡	游										
逮	捕										
刑	罚										
项	羽										

二 组词

轨_____ 巡_____ 巩_____ 纳_____

刑_____ 郡_____ 律_____ 逮_____

毁_____ 申_____ 廷_____ 币_____

三 选字组词

（申 伸）报　　（纳 内）税　　（项 顶）羽

（申 伸）手　　（纳 内）外　　山（项 顶）

朝（庭 廷）　　（征 证）服　　（亭 停）子

家（庭 廷）　　（征 证）明　　（亭 停）止

四 选择填空

1. 要参加夏令营的同学请马上去学校_____。

（报名　申报）

2. 公民应该自动_____并纳税。　　（报名　申报）

3. 秦始皇先后_____六国，统一了中国。

（佩服　征服）

4. 暴风雨过后，许多房屋被_____了。（烧毁　毁坏）

五 根据课文选择正确答案

1. 秦帝国是由_____建立的。

   A 周天子　　　　　B 秦王嬴(yíng)政　　　　C 秦孝公

2. 秦帝国是哪一年建立的？答：_____。

   A 2,000 年前　　　B 公元 221 年　　　　C 公元前 221 年

3. 秦帝国是中国历史上第一个统一的_____帝国。

   A 封建　　　　　　B 奴隶制　　　　　　C 民主制

4. 秦始皇修建了万里_____。

   A 灵渠　　　　　　B 阿房宫　　　　　　C 长城

5. _____是秦末农民起义的领导人。

   A 商鞅(yāng)　　　B 陈胜、吴广

六 词语解释

至高无上——

七 回答问题

1. 秦始皇推行了哪些政策？（写出五条）

_____

_____

_____

_____

_____

2. 你认为文字的统一对中国历史的发展有什么样的影响？

_____

_____

八 根据阅读材料判断对错

1. 秦统一六国前，匈奴人常闯入内地抢夺牛羊、粮食。　　___对　___错

2. 秦统一后，打败了匈奴，收回河套地区。　　___对　___错

3. 秦始皇用了十多年，将秦、赵、燕旧时的长城连接起来，建成了万里长城。　　___对　___错

4. 秦始皇兴修的宫殿中规模最大的是阿房宫。　　___对　___错

5. 秦始皇大军南下，为了运粮运兵，在今广东开凿灵渠。　　___对　___错

6. 灵渠沟通了长江水系和黄河水系。　　___对　___错

九　熟读课文

第六课

一 写生词

堤坝											
传播											
张仲景											
华佗											
疾病											
标志											
军阀											

二 组词

摆_____ 脱_____ 测_____ 堤_____

阀_____ 危_____ 镇_____ 播_____

管_____ 标_____ 免_____ 持_____

权_____ 疾_____ 疗_____ 染_____

三 选字组词

摆(脱 说)　　(提 堤)坝　　考(堤 题)

脱(鞋 蛙)　　(提 堤)包　　防水(堤 题)

监(侧 测)　　(镇 真)压　　传(翻 播)

(侧 测)面　　(镇 真)假　　(翻 播)译

传(梁 染)　　(治 冶)病　　治(疾 疗)

(梁 染)山　　(治 冶)炼　　(疾 疗)病

四 选择填空

1. 造纸术促进了文化的_____。(传播　传染)

2. 天气冷热变化大的时候,学校里常常会流行_____病。　　　　　　　　　　　　(传播　传染)

3. 中国的黄河常发洪水,所以要修好_____。
　　　　　　　　　　　　　　　　(堤坝　提水)

4. 蔡伦用树皮、破布为原料造纸,大大_____了成本。
　　　　　　　　　　　　　　　　(降低　削弱)

5. 这是一支现代化的_____。(军阀　军队)

6. 张衡制造了地动仪来_____地震。(监测　监狱)

五 根据课文判断对错

1. 东汉时期，蔡伦发明了用树皮、麻头、
   破布等造纸的方法。　　　　　　　___对　___错
2. 张衡制造了浑天仪和地动仪。　　　___对　___错
3. 《伤寒杂病论》是张仲景写的。　　___对　___错
4. 华佗发展了麻醉学和内科手术学。　___对　___错
5. 汉朝派班超出使西域。　　　　　　___对　___错
6. 东汉末年发生了"黄巾起义"。　　　___对　___错

六 造句

1. 杰出_____
2. 成就_____

七 词语解释

1. 显著——
2. 名存实亡——

八 回答问题

东汉时期,中国在科学技术上有哪些成就?

答:_____

_____

_____

_____

九 根据阅读材料选择正确答案

1. 华佗是东汉著名的医生,尤其精于_____。

   A 内科　　　B 外科　　　C 妇科　　　D 针灸科

2. 华佗让病人用酒喝下_____,等病人全身麻醉,就开刀做手术。

   A 菜汤　　　B 红酒　　　C 绿茶　　　D 麻沸散

3. 华佗在_____方面在世界医学史上有着重要的地位。

   A 外科和麻醉学　　　B 外科和内科　　　C 外科和妇科

4. 一次,华佗给关羽治病,要_____,再给他开刀治疗。

   A 盖住关羽的眼睛　　　B 给关羽喝"麻沸散"

5. 华佗给关羽刮骨时,关羽一边喝酒一边_____。

   A 哭叫　　　B 吃菜　　　C 看戏　　　D 下棋

6. 华佗说关羽是_____。

　　A 勇敢的人　　　　B 懒人　　　　C 神仙

十　熟读课文

第八课

一 写生词

汝	南	王								
奢	侈									
蜡										
陷	入									
刘	裕									
鲜	卑									
批	驳									
绘	画									

二 组词

奢_____ 卑_____ 融_____ 慰_____

批_____ 率_____ 陷_____ 绘_____

替_____ 迁_____ 彼_____ 伙_____

三 选字组词

（批 比）驳　　（迁 千）移　　（伙 火）食

评（批 比）　　（迁 千）万　　灭（伙 火）

（按 安）慰　　（绘 会）画　　奢（侈 多）

（按 安）照　　开（绘 会）　　希（蜡 腊）

四 给多音字注音

1. 祖冲之是世界上首先把圆周率（　　）推算到小数点后7位数的人。

2. 曹操率（　　）领20万大军南下。

五 选词填空

迁移　奢侈　交替　批评　安慰

1. 西晋时,贵族生活非常_____。

2. 许多高科技公司_____到中国和印度。

3. 妈妈常_____我做事马虎。

4. 春夏秋冬四季_____出现。

5. 李明生病了，朋友们都前去看望并且_____他。

六 根据课文选择正确答案

1. 西晋后期，为争夺皇位，出现了16年的混战，给人民带来_____。

   A 幸福　　　　B 灾难　　　　C 发展

2. 前秦皇帝苻(fú)坚率兵90万攻晋，东晋以8万兵迎击，战于淝(féi)水。最后，_____战败。

   A 东晋　　　　B 苻坚

3. 北魏孝文帝进行了使鲜卑族汉化的_____。

   A 方法　　　　B 战争　　　　C 改革

4. 两晋南北朝时期，战争连年，人民需要在痛苦中寻求安慰，因此_____流行。

   A 佛教、道教　　B 儒家思想　　C 天主教

5. 画家_____的名作《女史箴(zhēn)图》为传世珍品。

   A 王羲(xī)之　　B 祖冲之　　C 顾恺(kǎi)之

6. 王羲(xī)之是东晋时的_____。

   A 画家　　　　B 政治家　　　　C 书法家　　　　D 军事家

7. 南朝祖冲之是世界上第一个把圆周率推算到_____的人。

   A 小数点后3位数　　　B 7位数　　　C 小数点后7位数

七　根据阅读材料判断对错

1. 花木兰好读书，不喜欢骑马射箭。　　　___对　___错

2. 父亲年老不能当兵，木兰坐在计算机旁发愁叹气。　　　___对　___错

3. 木兰男扮女装替父从军。　　　___对　___错

4. 木兰买了马匹、马鞍、武器，告别了父母，上路打仗去了。　　　___对　___错

5. 晚上睡觉的时候，木兰想起了父母。　　　___对　___错

6. 皇帝要奖赏木兰，她只想要一匹千里马，好赶快回家。　　　___对　___错

7. 木兰回到家，换上了女装，同伴们看到一个美丽的姑娘。　　　___对　___错

八　熟读课文

第十课

一 写生词

谋	略										
教	授										
赋	税										
绢											
贞	观										
懦	弱										
唐	玄	宗									
驿	站										
聚	居										

二 组词

略____ 授____ 矩____ 懦____

策____ 灌____ 唯____ 僧____

聚____ 版____ 破____ 驿____

戚____ 贵____ 善____ 艰____

三 选字组词

（政　正）策　　（僧　曾）经　　（字　子）典

（政　正）确　　（僧　曾）人　　法（典　点）

教（授　受）　　灌（溉　概）

（授　受）到　　大（溉　概）

四 选择填空

1. 唐代制定了一部成文_____《唐律疏议》。

（字典　法典）

2. 唐太宗_____听取别人意见。（善于　善良）

3. 唐代_____繁荣，交通发达，以首都长安为中心有通向全国各地的道路。（工业　商业）

4. 唐朝打通了往来西域的道路,并使天山南北广大地区全部纳入唐朝的_____。(版图　图画)

5. 唐初,_____玄奘(zàng)到印度学习佛经,回国后把佛经翻译成汉语。(商人　僧人　军人)

五　选词填空

　　　　聚居　雄才大略　英雄　居民

1. 李世民是一个有_____的皇帝。

2. 每一个妈妈都是生活中的_____。

3. 旧金山的唐人街是华人_____的地方。

4. 本区的_____占全市人口总数的九分之一。

六　词语解释

　　雄才大略——

七　回答问题

　　1. 唐朝是哪一年建立的?

　　答:_____

2. 唐太宗的名字叫什么?

答:＿＿＿＿＿＿＿＿＿＿＿＿＿＿＿＿＿＿＿＿＿＿＿＿＿＿

3. 唐朝的首都在哪里?

答:＿＿＿＿＿＿＿＿＿＿＿＿＿＿＿＿＿＿＿＿＿＿＿＿＿＿

4. 唐太宗把文成公主嫁给了谁?

答:＿＿＿＿＿＿＿＿＿＿＿＿＿＿＿＿＿＿＿＿＿＿＿＿＿＿

5. 唐朝时中国有多少人口?

答:＿＿＿＿＿＿＿＿＿＿＿＿＿＿＿＿＿＿＿＿＿＿＿＿＿＿

6. 中国历史上唯一的女皇帝是谁?

答:＿＿＿＿＿＿＿＿＿＿＿＿＿＿＿＿＿＿＿＿＿＿＿＿＿＿

八 根据阅读材料选择正确答案

1. 玄奘是一位佛学大师、佛经翻译家和＿＿＿＿＿＿＿。

   A 文学家　　　　B 旅行家　　　　C 政治家

2. 公元627年,玄奘离开长安到＿＿＿＿＿＿＿取经。

   A 欧洲　　　B 印度　　　C 日本　　　D 越南

3. 玄奘西行前后 17 年,回到长安时带回 657 部 _____。

　　A 诗歌　　　　B 小说　　　　C 佛经

4. 玄奘回国后,翻译了大量梵(fàn)文经典,还将老子的 _____ 翻译成梵文。

　　A《圣经》　　B《道德经》　　C《可兰经》

5. 玄奘去印度取经,途经 138 国,后来把所见所闻写在 _____ 一书中。

　　A《大唐西域记》　　B《西游记》

6. 松赞干布是吐(tǔ)蕃(bō)国王,他娶了 _____ 的文成公主。

　　A 汉朝　　　B 秦朝　　　C 唐朝

7. 公元 641 年,文成公主入藏时带去了 _____ 等生产技术,还带去了种粮食、蔬菜的方法。

　　A 纺织、造纸　　B 打猎　　C 捕鱼

九　熟读课文

第二课听写

第四课听写

第六课听写

第八课听写

第十课听写

练习纸

中国历史(上)